MORE
POWER
TO YOU

MORE
POWER
TO YOU

ROBERT
COHEN

APPLAUSE
THEATRE & CINEMA BOOKS

More Power To You
By Robert Cohen
Text copyright © 2002 by Robert Cohen
Copyright © 2002 by Applause Theatre & Cinema Books
Designed by Lisa Vaughn, Two of Cups Design Studio, Inc.

Library of Congress Cataloging-in-Publication Data
Library of Congress Card Number: 2002104395

Printed in Canada

ISBN: 1-55783-456-3

APPLAUSE THEATRE & CINEMA BOOKS

151 W 46th Street, 8th Floor

New York, NY 10036

Phone: (212) 575-9265

Fax: (646) 562-5852

email: info@applausepub.com

www.applausepub.com

Sales & Distribution

NORTH AMERICA:

Hal Leonard Corporation
7777 West Bluemound Road
P.O. Box 13819
Milwaukee, WI 53213
Phone: (414) 774-3630
Fax: (414) 774-3259
email: halinfo@halleonard.com
internet: www.halleonard.com

UK:

Combined Book Services Ltd.
Units I/K, Paddock Wood
   Distribution Centre
Paddock Wood, Tonbridge,
Kent TN12 6UU
Phone: (44) 01892 837171
Fax: (44) 01892 837272
United Kingdom

for Lorna

C O N T E N T S

INTRODUCTION

I n the pages that follow you will find nineteen essays that I have written over the past forty years, half of which are concerned with playing and half on plays. There can be no suggestion that such a retrospective collection, "hic et ubique" as Hamlet might say, has a common theme, or even a common methodology, but it certainly does have a common origin: the sampling represents the composite of a scholarly and appreciative curiosity that, in my case at least, goes hand-in-glove with my long-standing (and ongoing) eagerness to make theatre: specifically to direct plays, and, if possible, to direct them well.

These pieces are, of course, not merely notes to myself. All but two of the essays have been previously published in journals or books, and I therefore would like to presume that they have even been read, at least by a few people, prior to the issuance of this edition. However, the diversity of the various fields of inquiry, and the four-plus decades they span, mean they have appeared in widely disparate publications with quite different readerships. I have a suspicion, thankfully shared by this volume's amazingly helpful and sensitive publisher, Glenn Young, that considering such a collage of theoretical, exegetic, and critical examinations side-by-side might define a certain professorial synergy in which the whole suggests more than the sum of its parts.

The broad diversity of approaches these works represent is neither coincidental nor unique. Directing plays, at least in the modern sense, is a relatively new theatre art, barely a century old; if we have any doubt of that we need only to look at Molière's depiction of his own directing ("Spread yourselves around!" he shouts to the actors) in his *Impromptu de Versailles.*

It was probably the realistic directors—Stanislavsky, the Duke of Saxe-Meiningen, André Antoine—who first sought to choose, and then forcefully impose, integrated and holistic conceptualizations of textual, visual, oral, and performative styles that would, in concert, shape individual play production before and around the turn of the last century. But when Gordon Craig proclaimed in his 1905 *Art of Theatre* the necessity of a directorial vision transcending a mere conformity to historical or psychological realism, the director of the 20th—and I dare say 21st—century was born. I and my directorial colleagues, therefore, through the pressure of professional competition if for no other reason, are now our own combinations of dramaturg, pedagogue, visualist, critic, composer, theorist, editor, acting coach, translator, and universal scholar of worldwide cultures, politics and traditions. The preparation necessary for effective and innovative directing always includes hard paddling in most if not all of these discrete but confluent waters.

You will, I hope, find some surprises in the pages that follow. In the essays, for example, you will read that Hamlet was sixteen, that Shakespeare's actors cried real tears and had several methods for doing so, that *Waiting For Godot* was based on the theology of a French Jewess, and that Jerzy Grotowski once admitted his Poor Theatre "always cost a lot of money." You will also find the secret whereby British actors walk off with the lion's share of Tony Awards, and why the kidnapped heiress Patty Hearst robbed a bank. If you don't agree with all of my premises, don't worry; most of the scholarly community doesn't either; yet there's nothing in this book that I have subsequently found reason to retract or significantly alter.

Compiling a book like this is both a pleasant and unsettling task; pleasant because there is a piquant nostalgia in ruminating over old discoveries and theatrical delights, unsettling because the dialectics I write of continue to reassert themselves in issues that have and can have no final resolution. Indeed, that's why theatre was created: to reassert, illuminate and vivify the uncertainties of existence. Writing about theatre— indeed, working in theatre, thinking about theatre, studying theatre, and above all attending the theatre—is to experience, always afresh and firsthand, the challenges of living, loving, and facing the often insurmountable challenges that we continually find in our paths.

SECTION 1 ONE

On Playing

CHAPTER

1

Tears (and Acting) in Shakespeare

Did Shakespeare's actors actually cry on stage? And if so, how did they manage to do it? And what might that say about the emotional "realism" of the acting in Shakespeare's company?

Characters shed tears throughout the canon; moreover, they do it while being observed by other characters. The words "weep" and "tears" appear more than 600 times in the plays, almost always in reference to someone sobbing in front of someone else: Othello, for example, weeps when he confronts Desdemona ("Am I the motive of these tears, my Lord?" she asks [IV.i.43]);[1] Menenius sobs before Coriolanus ("Thy tears are saltier than a younger man's," says Marcius [IV.i.22]); and Romeo wails in the Friar's cell ("There on the ground, with his own tears made drunk" complains the Friar [III.iii.83]). Often the sobbing is before a larger public: Claudio has "wash'd" Hero's foulness "with tears" in front of the whole wedding party (*Ado* IV.i.153-54); and Enobarbus weeps openly amidst Antony's brigade of also-sobbing soldiers ("Look, they weep, And I, an ass, am onion-eyed" [*A&C* IV.ii.341).

Sometimes the weeping is contagious, as in the ubiquitous lachrymosity of *Titus Andronicus*:

TITUS: . . . behold our cheeks how they are stain'd, like meadows yet not dry, with miry slime left on them by a flood? . . .

LUCIUS: Sweet father, cease your tears: for at your grief see how my wretched sister sobs and weeps.

MARCUS: Patience, dear niece. Good Titus, dry thine eyes.

TITUS: Ah, Marcus, Marcus, brother! well I wot thy napkin cannot drink a tear of mine, for thou, poor man, hast drown'd it with thine own.

LUCIUS: Ah, my Lavinia, I will wipe thy cheeks . . .

(III.i.136-39, 41-47)

Originally published in the *Journal of Dramatic Theory and Criticism*, Winter 1996

Occasionally, the weeping is from joy; not sadness. Timon cries with happiness during his first banquet ("Mine eyes cannot hold out water. methinks" [*Timon* I.ii.106-07]), provoking tears of sympathy from his guests ("Joy had the like conception in our eyes, and at that instant like a babe sprung up," says one [I.ii.108-09]), which Apemantus confirms with "Thou weepest to make them drink, Timon" (i. 109). Richard II cries in rapture before his whole kingdom:

> I weep for joy
> To stand upon my kingdom once again . . .
> As a long-parted mother with her child
> Plays fondly with her tears and smiles in meeting,
> So, weeping, smiling, greet I thee my earth . . .
>
> (III.ii.4-5, 8-10)

That Richard cries "as a . . . mother" implies a gender distinction in the act of crying, which is often present in the Shakespearean universe. When Flavius sobs, Timon looks at him in some astonishment: "What, dost thou weep? . . . Then thou art a woman and I love thee," (IV.iii.482-83). In Shakespeare's world, women are expected to cry and men are not. "Tears do not become a man." says Rosalind/Ganymede (*AYLI* III.vi.3), presumably addressing the issue on both sides of the gender divide. Contemporary studies indicate Shakespeare echoes a genuinely physiological gender trait.[2] Further Shakespearean examples are in the endnotes to this essay.[3]

But did the actors playing these parts produce real tears—meaning wet ones ("Be your tears wet?" Lear asks Cordelia [IV.vii.70], presumably determining the affirmative)—on stage? And if so, how did they accomplish this? By some sort of technical trick, or by somehow inducing a feeling of actual sadness?

Weeping real tears "on cue" is of course a very difficult feat: the physiology of crying is not subject to ordinary conscious control, particularly under the pressure and enhanced self-consciousness occasioned by public performance. But producing tears at the right moment has always been the acid test of the actor's art in emotional roles, known since ancient times as the only way to move the audience. Plato reported on the phenomenon in his *Ion* dialogue, where Ion, the famous rhapsode (reciter of poetry), tells Socrates that "[when I recite] the tale of pity my eyes are filled with tears" and goes on to say that his weepiness then produces "similar effects"[4] on his spectators. Ion's crying, Socrates guesses (and Ion confirms) comes from the performer's "inspiration," from having his "soul in an ecstasy," from being "out of his senses . . . out of [his] right mind."[5]

The acting maxim of Horace, in his subsequent *Ars Poetica*, was *si vis me flere, dolendum est primum ipsi tibi*: "If you would have me weep, you must first of all feel grief yourself."[6] Actors in the ancient world went to some extremes to "feel" this grief themselves. The Greek actor Polus grieved for his "Orestes," while playing Electra, by placing the urn of his real son's ashes on stage with him. The actors of the Renaissance had models, then, for crying onstage, and for stimulating these tears emotionally.

Certainly a verisimilitude of feeling was requisite in Elizabethan acting. With all the crying depicted and talked about onstage, and with the audience so close to the action (up to 3,000 people within 60 feet of the center of the action), the "crying" would appear ludicrous without glistening cheeks. John Webster defined "an excellent actor" by declaring that "what we see him personate, we think truly done before us,"[6] clearly implying a demand for performance that directly reflects the text. The anonymous eulogist of Richard Burbage, Shakespeare's leading actor, said of that great performer that the roles of Hamlet, Lear, Hieronomo, and Othello "lived in him," predating the Stanislavski dictum that the actor must "live the life of the character on stage" by three hundred years. In describing Burbage's Hamlet, the eulogist effused that:

> Oft have I seen him leape into a grave
> Suiting ye person (which he seemed to have)
> Of a sad lover, with so true an eye
> That then I would have sworn he meant to die . . .[8]

That "true eye" of Burbage/Hamlet must have been a wet one, as immediately thereafter Hamlet offers to compete with Laertes in a crying and fighting competition to determine who loved Ophelia most: "Woo't weep? woo't fight? . . . I'll do it." (V.i.272-73,76) Burbage cried, somehow, with Hamlet's tears. "I would have sworn he meant to die," said the eulogist of the actor. How did he do it?

There are several specific metatheatrical discussions in Shakespeare's plays describing characters who are themselves actors, or are acting or seeking to act, and who cry (or seek to cry) during the performance of "plays" within Shakespearean plays.

Shakespeare's first reference to "performed" crying is in *The Comedy of Errors*, and involves a crude gimmick: a manual massage of the tear glands. Shortly after Adriana promises to "weep what's left away, and weeping die;" she changes her mind: "No longer will I be a fool, / To put the finger in the eye and weep" (II.ii.203-04). Digital lacrimal duct stimulation can, in fact, set teariness aflow, and presumably that's what Adriana tries to do.

Falstaff, in improvising the "role" of King Henry at the Boar's Head, employs a biochemical stimulus to give the proper dimension to his performance: "Give me a cup of sack to make my eyes look red, that it may be thought I have wept, for I must speak in passion" (*1H4* II.vi.384-86), he commands. Apparently some sort of cognitive dissonance soon takes over the Knight, for by the end of the skit he admits to be crying indeed: "now I do not speak to thee in drink, but in tears" (II.vi. 414-15).[9] The mere appearance of weeping, together with the passion of the moment (and the headiness of the sack), has presumably lead to Falstaff's real (if unexpected) teariness.[10]

A different biochemical stimulus is employed in *The Taming of the Shrew*. In the play's induction, the First Lord asks his page, Bartholomew, to perform a woman's role in the play-within-the-play, suggesting that the lad employ, in the inevitable crying scene, a specific and time-tested technique:

> And if the boy have not a woman's gift
> To rain a shower of commanded tears,
> An onion will do well for such a shift,
> Which, in a napkin being close convey'd
> Shall in despite enforce a watery eye. (Ind.i.124-28)

The performer's "watery eye" can arrive either by "gift" or "shift," the Lord has made clear. But as the gift is strictly feminine (as women cry more often then men in Shakespeare's universe, as noted above), some special techniques must be employed by male actors—which, of course, means all the performers in Shakespeare's era. The Lord's "shift" is the hidden-onion trick, which in fact leaves the boy like Enobarbus, "onion-eyed," when he ("she") enters, "her" tears "like envious floods [having] . . . o'er-run her lovely face." (Ind.ii.64-65).

Physical/biochemical stimulations (and crying simulations) of Adriana, Falstaff, and Bartholomew are, of course, crude mechanical devices, even if, as in Falstaff's case, they lead to a deeper emotional acting "connection" to the "role." They have led some commentators to believe these were standard Elizabethan/Jacobean acting techniques, however, and that Shakespeare's professional actors employed like devices.[11]

But we must not forget that none of these three characters are actors. Falstaff, laments Mistress Quickly, "doth it as like one of these harlotry players as ever I see!" (II.vi.395). In no way are their techniques representative of the best stage acting methods in Shakespeare's time.

When Bottom the Weaver is asked—in *A Midsummer Night's Dream*—to prepare the "role" of Pyramus, he immediately realizes his greatest task: "That will ask some tears in the true performing of it . . . " (I.ii.25-26). As contrasted, Bottom must realize, to a *false* performing of it. Bottom's Pyramus is a "sad lover," as is Burbage's Hamlet in the eulogist's reference, and as a sad lover Bottom seeks the audience's empathy. Only his own tears, Bottom knows, will generate like tears from the audience: "If I do it [i.e. weep]," Bottom boasts, echoing Horace, "let the audience look to their eyes" (I.ii.26). Bottom indeed tries to evoke his tears when he gets to his epiphanic moment as Pyramus ("Come, tears, confound," Pyramus urges himself V.i.295]). Shakespeare doesn't let us know if the tears ever arrive (Bottom is an amateur, after all), but the task is clearly approached.

Bottom proposes a situationally related method to bring himself to teariness: "I will *condole* in some measure," the Weaver declares (I.ii.27). What Bottom refers to is what actors today call "playing an action;" specifically, in this case, the action of condolement, or grieving. Playing an action—one drawn from the play itself—is surely more emotionally consonant with the dramatic situation than poking a finger in the eye, quaffing a cup of sack, or secreting an onion in a napkin; it is also infinitely less cumbersome, requiring no hidden props or slight-of-hand. Moreover, it is an "inner" method, implying the actor perform with his own emotions, and, consequently, be "moved" in the same way as his character is, generating the same empathy described by Horace and others. The employment of a performed stage action, expressed in an active verb (to condole), becomes a durable link between actor and character; between, in this case, Bottom and Pyramus. Bottom will condole, Pyramus will cry, and the audience will look to their eyes. Thus does an actor's (own) self-expression (and resultant emotionality) combine with the mimesis of character simulation (text, gesture, costume) to equal theatre magic. Action—or, as we often say today, "playing the verb"—is a more useful, and convenient acting technique than digital or biochemical manipulation of the actor's physiology.

But for what (or over whom) does Bottom condole? For an imaginary dead-Thisbe? Or for an imagined-dead "Flute," (the character who plays the role of Thisbe)? Or does the actor playing Bottom grieve, in imagination, for an imagined-dead Thomas

Pope, who (possibly) was the actor playing the role of Flute-playing-Thisbe? Or did the actor playing Bottom condole for something/someone else altogether? Someone in his real life, as the actor Polus did with his own son? In sum: if "condole" is the verb, what is its object?

Bottom doesn't say, and, in this play at least, Shakespeare doesn't either. To do so would be to leave the light-hearted comedy of *A Midsummer Night's Dream* and negotiate through the multiple paradoxes of acting theory.[12]

In *Hamlet*, which is a play about (among other things) acting, Shakespeare portrays an actor crying in much greater detail. When the Player delivers Aeneas' speech (presumably from a version of "Dido and Aeneas"), Polonius (an amateur actor himself) is amazed to see the Player cry real tears, exclaiming, "Look! where he has not turned his color and has tears in's eyes!" (II.ii.519-20). Apparently the old counsellor is so alarmed (or piqued by the professional's skill) that he makes the Player cease "acting" on the spot. Clearly, the Player is a virtuoso of his craft. Alone, Hamlet soon meditates upon this player and this event:

HAMLET: Is it not monstrous, that this player here,
But in a fiction, in a dream of passion,
Could force his soul so to his own conceit,
That from her working all the visage wanned,
Tears in his eyes, distraction in's aspect,
A broken voice, and his whole function suiting
With forms to his conceit? (II.ii.550-57)

As Ion was "out of his . . . right mind" so the Player was "in a dream of passion," and thus able to "force his soul" into a physiological state ordinary persons cannot will themselves into. But this is, at the moment, "monstrous" in Hamlet's mind, and for two reasons: first, because Hamlet cannot so force his soul ("I know not seems," the character had earlier claimed [I.ii.76]); and second, because acting itself is, in Hamlet's terms, a Satanic conceit. Only "the dev'l hath power / T'assume a pleasing shape," Hamlet will say (II.ii. 598-89). It was the Duke of Gloucester, soon to be the "monstrous" Richard III, who claimed he could "wet my cheeks with artificial tears, / And frame my face to all occasions." [*III Henry VI*, III.ii.184-85.) That acting—the contrived simulation of feelings—is monstrous is a traditional medieval and Renaissance assumption.[13] The Greeks, after all, called the actor *hypokrite*. Even Plato, while admiring it, condemned it morally.[14] Bottom, when offering to play the role of Thisbe, realizes he will have to "speak in a monstrous little voice" (I.ii.52). But forcing the soul into the "conceit" (contrivance) of a written text and premeditated directorial instructions is the traditional soul of acting; a Neitzschean synthesis by which drama's Dionysian expression and ecstasy is marshalled (and this is the "conceit") into suitably Appollonian "forms."

Acting is monstrous, to Hamlet, but also essential: before he can become a king, or kill a king, he somehow must be able to "act" a king, and act a king-killer; he must, like the actor, learn to unleash his powers and act on his feelings. (The Prince must become a Player—in both the classic and the modern sense). Thus the Prince's celebrated dalliances with the Elizabethan players are no mere diversions, they are part and parcel of Hamlet's learning process, a sequence of "rehearsals" that will, during the course of the play, teach him how to play Dido, how to play Pyrrhus, how to play Lucianus, and how, finally, to play (and then to become, to declare himself) "Hamlet the Dane," revenger of his father's murder, and heir to his father's title. (Hamlet claims this title while leaping into Ophelia's grave—and crying.) In *Hamlet,* therefore, Shakespeare embarks on an inclusive—if abbreviated—analysis of acting, beginning with the metonymic problem of tears on cue. But how does he get into the player's "dream of passion?" It is the same way that Stanislavski was later to describe: through *motivation.*

> . . . What would he [the Player] do
> Had he the motive and the cue for passion That I have?
> He would drown the stage with tears . . .
> (II.ii.560-62)

The sentence incorporates three key words of Shakespeare's—and more recent—acting theory: motive, cue, and passion. With *motive,* Hamlet recognizes that acting—and action ("what would he *do*")—must spring from a motivation; and consequently that crying—which is an action—must have a motivationally inciting force. It is not a unique discovery in Shakespeare ("Am I the motive of these tears, my Lord?" Desdemona asks Othello [IV.i.43]), but an important one. Motive, etymologically, is the animating propulsion, the "motor," of both conscious and unconscious human behavior. It is also the engine of *emotion*; indeed, these two words have a common root (Latin: *emovere*), reflecting the medieval and Renaissance belief that human feelings result from actual movements of bodily fluids: the "humours" (blood, phlegm, bile, and tears) and/or "vital spirits" whose travel through the body links affect to behavior, and propels feeling into action. Current physiology accepts this, although the terminologies have been changed to neural transmissions, hormonal flows, and the chemical homeostasis and imbalances that generate emotional behavior.

But the fluid mechanics of the stage are, by necessity, *the actor's, not the character's*. Only the actor's blood (and phlegm, bile, neurons, and hormones) can actually move; only the actor has a character's "chemistry." The character, prior to the performance, is merely a literary artifact. The Player knows this, and so "moves" himself to deep feeling (and therefore effective persuasion) by wholly absorbing Aeneas' (and through Aeneas,' Hecuba's) motive. Through the Player's "acting," and pursuit of the Aeneas' (the character's) motive, he (the Player) becomes emotionally powerful and rhetorically intense. These are lessons Hamlet needs to learn himself.

Thus a notion of character "motivation"—rather than mere external theatrical imperative—appears implicitly in Shakespeare as the linchpin of effective acting. That Stanislavski elaborated on this idea three centuries later in no way suggests it was the Russian director/teacher's invention.

Hamlet has his motivation, and his "cue for passion" which should trigger it, but unlike the Player he cannot yet "act"; something is still missing. And Hamlet knows what it is.

Yet I,
A dull and muddy-mettled rascal, peak
Like John-a-dreams, unpregnant of my cause
And can say nothing . . . (II.ii.566-69)

Hamlet still finds himself where the Ghost had warned earlier: "duller . . . than the fat weed / That roots itself in ease on Lethe wharf" (I.v.32-33). He is like John-a-Dreams, not in a dream of passion. He can "say nothing" and, unlike the Player, he cannot drown the stage with tears even when he tries ("O Vengeance! / Why what a fool am I"). The reason: Hamlet's motivation to act is powerful, his cue for passion has arrived, but he is unpregnant of a *cause*. Motivation and cause, though often used interchangeably, refer to wholly different temporal perspectives. Motivation stems from events in the past; cause leans aggressively into the future. Cause includes a goal as well as a rationale; it integrates energy with analysis: it races towards its own completion as much as it serves as a point of departure. Cause provides the force and focus of action; it becomes the "higher calling" that makes action become surrational and (dramatically) inevitable; it provides the specific direction for motive, giving it focus and a future expectation. While a cue can compress the fires of feeling into a timed explosion, cause can put that explosion into a rifle's barrel. Cue fires the powder; cause selects the target and aims the gun. "I'll be an auditor. An actor too, if I see cause," puns Puck (*MSND* III.i.80).

And now we must see beyond the peculiarity of the phrase "*unpregnant* of my cause." The cause that Hamlet seeks—and which the Player has—is not merely intellectual, and it cannot be acquired through merely rational means. True passion-animating cause enters the body not through the head but through the viscera; its assault is sexual, biotic, and corporally transporting. The great actor (as well as the great tragic hero) is *pregnant* with cause: cause has become the seed of a new life within and a new power without. Transcending merely rational, or Horatian, or even Apollonian models, Shakespeare reaches down to the carnal—and up to the spiritual—realms of Dionysus. Acting, in the Hamlet model, synthesizes earthly fertility and divine rapture. The great actor does indeed ape the monstrous, and becomes, in the French phrase, a *monstre sacré*, on a plane beyond both the mortal and the quotidian. But he/she also becomes the new life force: reproductive and fecund. And when the (male) actor becomes pregnant with (his character's) cause, gender limitations disappear: the male assumes the "woman's gift," along with the male's, and cries and fights (as one "splenetive and rash" [*Ham.* V.i.261]) in an androgynous, self-fertilizing consummation, one (perhaps) devoutly to be wished. Cause has become, as an embryo, a new and inner life, growing within the body; maturing, assuming an independent existence; joining with the character to become the actor's alter-ego. It is the ecstasy of play transmogrified (suited) into the formalism of *the* play. It is Burbage's emotion shaped into a Hamlettian mimesis.

The preceding paragraph extends, of course, into speculation and perhaps meditation (if not whimsy). It is of no consequence in the vast critical literature on *Hamlet*. But I think it touches on clear indications from Shakespeare as to the life of the actor, the actor (Burbage) in whom Hamlet lived, and to the emotion that great actors feel when these parts live in them, and their tears flow from them.

NOTES

1   All citations from *The Riverside Shakespeare*, G. Blakemore Evans, ed., (Boston: Houghton Mifflin, 1974.).

2   Women cry more in real life too. Dr. William H. Frey II at the Ramsey Clinic Dry
     Eye and Tear Research Center in St. Paul, Minnesota, has determined that boys and
     girls up to the age of twelve cry with equal frequency, but by age eighteen, women cry
     almost four times as frequently as men. Frey determines that there is a biological basis
     as well as psychological: emotional tears contain the hormone prolactin which aids
     milk production. By the age of eighteen, women have 60% more prolactin than men.
     Frey finds that women cry an average of 5.3 times a month; men 1.4 times a month.
     Los Angeles Times, D-1, February 2, 1994.

3   Women in Shakespeare cry much more freely and frequently than men. Virgilia weeps
     more than she speaks in *Coriolanus.* Lavinia's "fresh tears" (III.i.111) remain mute testi-
     mony to her ravaged body long after her violation in *Titus* ("thou hast no hands to
     wipe away thy tears," Titus mourns [III.i.106]). Lady Anne "pour[s] the helpless balm
     of [her] poor eyes" onto her late uncle's corpse in *Richard III* (I.2.13). Lady Beatrice
     has been weeping onstage "all this while" when Benedick accosts her in *Much Ado*
     (IV.i.255). And Lord Capulet jocularly confronts the sobbing Juliet ("blubb'ring and
     weeping, weeping and blubb'ring,") after describing her (at III.iii.87) in a staggering
     series of watery metaphors: "It rains downright! / How now, a conduit, girl? What! still
     in tears? / Evermore showering? . . . For still thy eyes, which I may call the sea, / Do
     ebb and flow with tears" (III.v.128-30,32-33). And poor blubbering Cordelia cries in
     every act of *King Lear* in which she appears: "With washed eyes / Cordelia leaves you"
     she tells her sisters in Act One (I.i.268-89); "Be your tears wet?" her father queries in
     Act Four (IV.vii.70); "Wipe thine eyes," Lear begs her in Act Five (V.iii.13). Male
     tears, when they come, generally appear as an undesirable effeminacy. Romeo's tears,
     says the Friar, are "womanish" (III.iii.110): "unseemly woman in a seeming man" (I.
     112). "Lend me fool's heart and a woman's eyes," says Timon to the Senators, "and I'll
     beweep these comforts" (V.i.157-58). Wolsey tells Cromwell, "I did not think to shed a
     tear / In all my miseries; but thou has forced me, / Out of thy honest truth, to play the
     woman. Let's dry our eyes . . . " (*HVIII* III.ii.429-31.) Lear scorns tears as "women's
     weapons, water drops" (II.vi.275); though, in the end, he can't restrain them. Likewise,
     Laertes tries to hold back his tears but fails, and this "trick" of nature shames his
     would-be masculinity:

>   I forbid my tears: but yet
>   It is our trick, nature her custom holds,
>   Let shame say what it will. When these are gone,
>   The woman will be out. (*Ham* IV.vii.186-89)

4   Ion to Socrates; in Cole, Toby and Chinoy, Helen, eds., *Actors on Acting* (New York: Crown, 1970), p.8. Shakespeare also demonstrates this process in *Two Gentlemen of Verona* when Julia, pretending to be Sebastian, tells Sylvia about how she had once acted "Julia" playing the role of "Ariadne" before Julia herself. The speech is a lie, but the process described is (and must be) obviously credible:

> And at that time I made her weep agood,
>
> For I did play a lamentable part.
>
> Madam, 'twas Ariadne passioning
>
> For Theseus' perjury and unjust flight;
>
> Which I so lively acted with my tears
>
> That my poor mistress, moved therewithal,
>
> Wept bitterly. (IV.iv.170-71.)

5   Ibid.

6   Ibid. 88.

7   Ibid. 88.

8   Ibid. 90.

9   The same effect occurs in Master Postast, the Poet, in the anonymous and undatable *Histriomastix* who calls for wine (Canadoe) to aid him in rehearsing a prologue (in bold type), and, after drinking it, resumes his rehearsal of his text:

> **My Son, thou art a lost child,**
>
> (This is passion, note you the passion?)
>
> **And hath many poor men of their goods beguiled:**
>
> **Oh, prodigal child, and child prodigal . . .**
>
> **Read the rest, sirs, I cannot read for tears.**

Mann, David, *The Elizabethan Player,* (New York: Routledge, 1991) 162.

10 There is a long history of actors simulating emotion technically, and then finding that they "feel" the feelings technically simulated. This became one of the central theme of Stanislavski's "Theory of Physical Actions," and is perhaps best expressed by the dictum of the late American director William Ball: "Do the act, the feeling will follow."

11 Meredith Anne Skura states that "Shakespeare's actors sawed the air with oratorical flourishes and used conventional gestures to express fear, anger, love or other passions," and that "the dizzying repertory schedule which required [one of Shakespeare's actors] to keep several such roles in mind at once ought, we now feel, to preclude any psychological involvement with the characters he played." (*Shakespeare: The Actor and the*

Purposes of Playing, [University of Chicago Press, 1993, p. 49]). Skura defends this position, which I'm afraid I find untenable, by noting that "Falstaff used an onion [*sic.,* actually it was a cup of sack] rather than a sad memory to make his eyes red," and footnotes that the Page in Shrew is directed to use an onion as well. (Ibid). However, Skura ignores the fact that neither Falstaff nor the Lord's Page are actors, nor is the Lord (who "directs" his page) a theatrical coach or director. Lacking any theatrical technique whatever, Falstaff, Page, and Lord must of course employ such gimmicks. And no modern actor would suggest that a repertory schedule would preclude psychological involvement with his or her characters. Quite to the contrary, my experience indicates that such emotional involvement is virtually essential for an actor to quickly differentiate his or her roles from each other, and energize each with the requisite passion and intensity.

12 A survey of these paradoxes is artfully laid out in Joseph Roach, *The Player's Passion: Studies in the Science of Acting*, (University of Delaware Press, 1985).

13 "The Devil was widely considered to be the best actor, precisely because he lacked the personal integrity that inhibits or modifies impersonation," concludes David Mann, surveying Renaissance literature on the subject. In *The Elizabethan Player*, (New York: Routledge, 1991) 96.

13 The literature is fully surveyed in Jonas Barish, *The Anti-theatrical Prejudice* (Berkeley: University of California Press, 1981).

CHAPTER

2

Dragging Carcasses to the Firepit: Acting Theory, Practice, and Pedagogy

Why should acting students hate acting theory? Perhaps they're simply impatient to get to the business at hand. Or worried that the act of thinking about acting will make them uncomfortably self-conscious in performance. Or perhaps they've seen too many television interviews where a movie star preens his or her "untaught genius" to an adoring public.

In any event, many of our students do hate theory, sometimes for legitimate reasons. So do some acting teachers, who implore their charges with the classic directive, "Don't think about it, just DO it!" But purposeful and discreet theorizing, I believe, is integral to some of the best teaching—and best learning—of acting.

Theory (from the Greek: *theoria*: the act of viewing, contemplation) is simply a way of seeing things. If we assume that life is a near-infinite aggregation of perceived phenomena, then theorizing is simply the act of seeing, and then organizing, some of those apparent phenomena in such a way as to establish some general—and, one hopes, useful—principles.

Take, for an example of the latter, the caveman who, pulling a mammoth's carcass over a broken-off tree limb and watching it glide over the rolling limb, came up with a "wheel theory" and thereby invented the wheel. This surely provided him practical benefits; and by communicating the theory to his descendants, he insured that future generations would not have to "reinvent the wheel," which conveyed practical benefits to them as well. We might remember, in this context, that the Mayan civilization, though building great pyramids, never discovered the wheel. Presumably, Mayan stonemasons simply yelled at their slaves, "Don't think about it, just MOVE it!"

Theorizing of this sort is not merely an abstract pastime, nor just a form of mental entertainment. It is thinking that is communicable, that builds from learned principles, that moves from the simple to the complex, and that organizes perceptions

Originally published in the *Theatre Topics*, September 1995 and experience into lasting and practical strategies. It is thus particularly effective in teaching because it organizes pedagogy with an aligned, focused perspective—a "way of seeing"—which can become the basis of a systematic approach. And a systematic approach—in contrast to a purely experiential one—can be divided into discrete units and structured into a series of graduated steps, leading to an educational process. This is pedagogically sound, since we learn most complex tasks processionally, i.e., step by step. No one would expect a student to understand calculus without first learning algebra, or understand algebra without first learning arithmetic, or learn arithmetic before mastering numbers. Acting, though more art than science, is similarly learned through a graduated process: a procession of incremental advances.

There are, of course, nonsystematic modes of instruction. In acting, after-the-fact criticism, or "critiquing," is one of these: an acting task is assigned, the instructor "critiques" the effort, and the student tries again. The two major problems with such critiques may be stated quickly:

(1) The student, in adjusting his/her work to meet the demands of the critique, has neither necessarily acquired any tools by which improvement can be made in future tasks, nor necessarily encountered any general principles for evaluating progress in such tasks.

(2) The critique may be highly subjective and idiosyncratic. Moreover, as no theoretical principles are engaged, there is no way to test the critique's objectivity, universality, or general effectiveness, leaving the instructor generally unaccountable for the student's further progress.

Critiquing is often employed for no more reason than it is easy to do, requires no advance preparation, is hard to challenge empirically, and is usually high-sounding, with the implicit framing of "I'm right, you're wrong." Inasmuch as critiques privilege the teacher, they marginalize the student. In the study of acting, particularly, critiquing can stultify creativity without necessarily elevating standards of art, craft, or discipline. While a critique may solve immediate and closely defined problems, it may produce little or no growth in a student's long-range artistic development.

Pedagogy founded on a communicated theoretical base, however, may have more long-lasting value, both as a means of instruction and as a support for artistry and the free-flow of creative imagination. It may pay other dividends as well. Well-defined and well-conveyed acting theory provides motivation and discipline to artistic and intellectual processes. It provides a language for artistic and intellectual collaboration.

It lends structure to creativity and confidence to imagination. It leads to intellectual connections with other thinkers—in and out of the theatre—and to other modes of thought. It dignifies the process it informs and intensifies the student's search for artistic value. It is a strong basis for further growth.

I should make clear, however, that I am speaking of *practical* theorizing. Practical theorizing is what the first wheel theorist employed: it entails finding real solutions to real and necessary questions, such as: how big should a wheel be? If the wheel's too large, it gets weighed down in the mire; if it's too small, it stalls in the ruts; if it's too wide, it encounters too many stones along its path; if it's too narrow, it will snap in two when turned too sharply. The first successful wheel theorist, backed by a history of hundreds of real wheels, had to make a practical calculus that led to a wheel's optimum parameters. Wheel theory is eminently pragmatic; it derives from experience and follows rather than precedes actual practice. There were lots of wheels, and lots of them failed, before there were successful wheel theories or wheel theorists.

Projective theory is somewhat different. Projective theories extend to problems that don't necessarily exist, or don't yet exist, or haven't yet been identified. Projective theories may not even address problems at all, but merely pose the potential interplays (and derived ironies) of phenomena not previously thought of as meriting such pointed juxtaposition. Einstein's Theory of Relativity was a famous projective theory, although the passage of time has made it a practical one as well. Poststructuralist literary theory began, for the most part, as projective philosophizing, although subsequent research and experience has in many cases led to real-world applications.

Projective theory is usually popular in the academy, often for the same reasons that critiquing is: it's easy to do, hard to challenge, and almost invariably high-sounding. And very little of it is held accountable, even by its proponents, for immediate or measurable results. This may not be problematic in literary or philosophical circles, where elegant abstraction has an aesthetic of its own, but it does raise some legitimate hackles in the area of dramatic performance, since the theatre provokes an immediate, quantifiable, and public response, e.g., applause, tears, gasps, and laughter—plus the possibility of press reviews, fan mail, box office revenue, private donations, and/or foundation grants. The theatre, as an immediate, public, and practical art, has proven traditionally inhospitable to anything that might appear as abstract intellectualizing, and projective theorizing has been broadly satirized, as a sort of pompous buffoonery, by theatrical greats from Aristophanes to Shakespeare to Molière to Pirandello. The actual art of acting—as opposed to the philosophical role of the actor—has therefore remained somewhat immune to contemporary projective or "critical" theorizing. Certainly, as the late Robert Corrigan was fond of saying, "no one has ever discovered how to deconstruct an actor."

I will limit myself in this essay, therefore, to elaborating only on the virtues of practical theory, which I would like to illustrate with a class exercise I call "I Hate Monday." The exercise is deceptively simple: with the class arranged in a circle, student participants simply memorize and speak—one at a time, while looking into each other's eyes—the following text: "I hate Monday, I hate Tuesday, I hate Wednesday, I hate Thursday, I hate Friday, I hate Saturday, I hate Sunday."

Without my suggesting it, interpersonal acting goals (or "character" objectives) quickly assert themselves. Speakers may, for example, use the text to solicit pity from the hearers. Or they try to amuse the hearers with the mock-magnitude of their increasingly eloquent despair. Yet, since the hearers don't immediately respond with pity, or amusement, the speakers' goals remain unfulfilled, which forces them to "try harder" with every phrase of the speech. This "builds" the speech: ordinarily in volume, in sharpness of diction, and/or in emotional intensity. Pretty soon we are hearing, instead of the flat initial reading, something like:

I hate Monday,
I hate Tuesday,
I hate Wednesday,
I hate Thursday,
I hate Friday,
I hate Saturday
I hate Sunday!!

I encourage this structural progression, mainly by asking the speakers to make clear to the hearers that they hate "Tuesday" more than "Monday," and "Wednesday" more than "Tuesday," and so forth. Then I channel this progression into a more structured pattern by asking the speakers to make clear that they hate each of the first six days by the same margin more than they hate the last one: for example, that they hate "Tuesday" 10% more than "Monday" and "Wednesday" 10% more than "Tuesday," etc. In that way, something of an acting "ladder" is built with equidistant—and therefore easy-to-climb—steps.

Finally, I ask that the speakers make clear that they hate "Sunday" more than "Saturday" by an even greater margin: that, for example, if each of the first six days is hated 10% more than the previous one, "Sunday" is hated 20% more, or 50% more. Indeed, "Sunday" is virtually "off the scale" in its hatefulness!

This results in a mounting escalation of steadily rising steps through the first six days of the week and a virtual explosion of feeling on the seventh. The rising action from Monday to Saturday provides a momentum of interest and promises some sort of conclusion, since nothing can build forever. It conveys a sense of urgency and encourages interpersonal contact (even interpersonal penetration) between the speaker and the hearers—particularly when the speaker catches the hearers with direct eye contact. And the ensuing dramatic potential virtually erupts in the "off-the-scale" explosion on "Sunday," which creates a satisfying and sometimes thrilling closure to the "speech."

Closure, however, is not merely a rhythmic or technical crescendo: it also points to a subtext beneath the argument, suggesting that the "hatred" is not actually of the individual days, which are, after all, only the nominal integers of a week, but to certain unconscious or sublimated targets; for example: "I hate [the person I'm usually with on] Monday, I hate [the person I'm usually with on] Tuesday . . .," etc. It also may provoke strong subtextual interrelationships between the speaker and the hearers: "I hate [the person I'm usually with, and YOU know who THAT is, on] Monday . . .," etc. Thus these purely structural characteristics may produce a powerful dramaturgical impact, giving the speech direction and the sense of a target, giving it interactive force and communicable subtext, and investing the speaker/character with a high dramatic promise or potential. In such cases, they then also provide an emotional and aesthetic propulsion, a musicality (sometimes a quite thunderous musicality) which can, in its fullest expression, lead to a state of rapturous excitement: as musical codas provide in Beethoven symphonies, or the Dies Irae of Verdi's Requiem, or the instrumental tag to the Beatles' "A Day in the Life." Heady stuff for a brutally simple and seemingly content-free "exercise."

But the questions surely arise in the students' minds: Why does/should a *character* (as opposed to the actor, or the playwright, or the director) build a speech? Is speech-building an organic characteristic of real-world human behavior, or is it a mere theatrical technique, a mathematical/musical/aesthetic device for stimulating the audience? These are good questions, which require some elemental and practical theorizing.

Speeches build for at least two reasons: (1) they comprise an architecture of mutually dependent arguments; and/or (2) their preliminary steps fail to achieve their goal, requiring an escalation of effort. Both of these reasons, however, depend on the actor—on behalf of the character—truly trying to convince (persuade, affect, solicit, amuse) *other* people. Rote-recited texts, such as the classroom "Pledge of Allegiance," do not build when normally spoken—even though they are rhetoricaliy structured to do so—simply because they are not addressed to anyone and not intended by their speakers to convince anyone. Interpersonal, goal-driven, objective-powered speeches *do* build in real life because in such cases the speaker is trying to achieve something (usually something difficult) with each phrase. And they build until the speaker either succeeds in achieving his/her goal, or gives up and tries something else. Students who understand this rather primitive—but crucial—theoretical principle have a much easier time handling the technical aspects of speech building than those who are simply told "just DO it!" I follow the "I hate Monday" exercise with a discussion of "speech building theory," exploring how speeches build in everyday life, and how they also fulfill a dramaturgical function.

I then return to the exercise, substituting an alternate verb into the text: "I love Monday, I love Tuesday . . . "or sometimes "I worship Monday, I worship Tuesday. . ." Here the specific acting goal shifts: perhaps to eliciting enthusiasm from fellow lovers or worshipers, or sharing one's rapture towards a group religious ecstasy. The "build" in these cases goes in a radically different sort of direction than in the "I hate" version, but *the speech builds nonetheless.* Having failed to elicit the proper enthusiasm or rapture on one phrase, the speakers must "try harder" on each successive one, "superescalating" the build on "Sunday." Indeed, the climax in the "I love" variation may be even more apocalyptic—though usually much quieter—than in the "I hate" original. It quickly becomes clear that there is a direct parallelism of escalation to closure between the "I hate" and "I love" builds. In no case can closure occur unless the "Sunday" goes suffi-ciently overscale to bring the list to a satisfying conclusion. But "Sunday" cannot go overscale unless there IS a scale to go over, which can only occur if the previous days are built in a regular and controlled escalation.

But now we come to a reversal of focus in this exercise. Employing the rhetorical structure of escalation is only half the challenge of "I hate/love Monday"; the other, equally important, is to *individuate the days.* For, to the character speaking, "Thursday" must not merely be 10% more hated than "Wednesday"; "Thursday" must also be a *real day* in which real things happen or could happen. Playwrights may create drama-turgy, but actors must create personal and human experience. Neither "Monday" nor "Thursday" may be reduced by an actor to a mere rhetorical cipher in the greater structural account of the week. Nor, in a production that aspires to probe human depth or complexity, may a character appear merely as some sort of dramaturgical construct. While textual structure may propel dramatic momentum, the *authenticity* of each individual step within that structure determines the actor's credibility as a human being. Dramatic momentum is comprised of moment-to-moment and personal authenticity, which must be laid down in the individuation of a play's discrete units. In my view, it is only in the total fusion of these elements—overall structure and moment-to-moment individuation—that we can find great theatre.

But achieving both of these goals—the individuation of the days and the "ladder" of the week—and achieving them simultaneously, is decidedly NOT a simple task for the actor. Indeed, it is a deeply bifurcated task, since its two goals are apparently contradictory: over-individuation obscures the pattern, while overpatterning strips its separate integers of authenticity.

Let's look at this in an actual dramatic text. Desdemona's speech to Othello, urging her husband to a reconciliatory meeting with Cassio, is structurally parallel to the exercise text:

Why then, tomorrow night, on Tuesday morn,
On Tuesday noon, or night, on Wednesday morn,
I prithee name the time, but let it not
Exceed three days . . . (*Othello* III.iii.60-63)

It is the build in this speech that gives it its urgency. As Desdemona successively fails to arrange the meeting (Othello remaining silent all the while), she must work harder and harder to come up with a winning proposal. Yet Cassio's situation—and perhaps hers as well—is becoming more precarious with each of her failures to do so. It is with increasing desperation, therefore, that she offers specific meeting times until finally, realizing her build of specific demands is going nowhere, she abandons this tactic and retreats to pleading ("I prithee") for a much more general commitment ("within three days"). Desdemona's speech might build, therefore, something like the "Monday" exercise:

Why then, tomorrow night,
on Tuesday morn,
on Tuesday noon,
or night,

on Wednesday morn, I prithee
NAME THE TIME—
but let it not exceed three days . . .

Yet while the structural build in the speech lends it momentum and compulsion, Desdemona (the character) doesn't want to "build a speech," she wants to arrange a meeting—which she fails to do. And the "tomorrow night" that she initially proposes is, for her, a real date and time: she can imagine just where they would be coming from, where they would meet, and what they would do; perhaps, for example, she had planned a dinner party for tomorrow night which she would now be willing to forgo. Then, when Othello by his silence rejects "tomorrow night," she must "try harder" by offering "Tuesday morn"—another real moment in time, at which, perhaps, Desdemona would have to get up earlier than she would like and forgo the breakfast in bed with her new husband she had hoped to have. And so on. These or other actor choices provide both texture and personal authenticity to each of Desdemona's "meeting time" proposals, and—though the audience could not possibly "read" them for their specific content—flesh out the character from the text: a "real" person would be making a "real" offer and a "real" sacrifice with each of these proposals. It is Desdemona's (the character's) hope and belief that Othello might accept "tomorrow night," or at least "Tuesday morn," or then at least "Tuesday night"—were she only persuasive enough to convince him—that serves to make Desdemona (the actor) appear as a credible and sympathetic character. If, on the other hand, Desdemona were seen as simply creating a structured rhetorical build of various dates, she would be seen merely as a manipulative wife. So, for reasons of character credibility, the actor playing Desdemona must convince us of Desdemona's genuine hope of arranging a meeting, and her belief that she has a good chance of doing so, at every step: even Desdemona's proffer of "Wednesday morn," coming after four rejections, must have (in the character's mind) a chance of success—or Desdemona would not propose it.

By looking at this example closely (i.e., by theorizing) we clearly see that both the dramatic structure and the individuation of text elements—the rhetorical pattern and the authenticity of the individual units, the momentum of the text and the "moments" of the actor—must become inextricably linked in performance. Structure defines limits and parameters. Unlike life, a play is an organized series of finite events; it flows along a defined vector of space and time, and is headed towards some sort of collective and simultaneous conclusion. While a life, say, lasts seventy-five years or so, ending randomly and arbitrarily, a play lasts but two and a half hours, and its final curtain comes down—at a predetermined moment—simultaneously for actors and audience alike. Out of that final moment, and in its focus and compression of a theatrical pattern, comes—if not a message—then a paradigm, a model, an aesthetic, a perspective, a new lucidity over existence.

But the play's structure does not exist separately from the characters' individual actions and the trajectories they inscribe. Indeed, dramatic structure is comprised of the interplay of such trajectories. And the integrity of a play's overall structure is based in large measure on the human integrity of each action within it. That is, the rhetorical structure must be clearly linked to characters' pursuit of what I have here called goals and what Stanislavsky first called (as translated by Hapgood, 105-19) "objectives." Stanislavsky's terminology is useful here because if a character's objective links to the individuation of steps on a rhetorical ladder, a character's "super-objective" (Hapgood, 256-65) links to the overall structure of a speech, or a scene, or a play. Stanislavsky understood as well as any rhetorician the relationship of structure to individuation and was particularly adept at eliciting a thunderous musicality from the patterning of discrete and authentic character interactions. (Stanislavsky was trained, of course, as an opera singer.) Some basic theorizing about the rhetoric of performance can therefore tie us into the Russian master's system—to the extent we may find this useful.

For me, the combination of dissimilar (and in some ways seemingly contradictory) tasks makes "I Hate/Love Monday" a particularly challenging and eye-opening exercise. Students with strong naturalistic training or instincts will often opt for deep (and increasingly "clever") individuation of the separate days. Conversely, students with musical backgrounds may tend to emphasize the ladder (the structure) without much attention to the steps that make it up. Working with the latter problem, I often have the students perform the exercise while walking around the circle, pointing at persons who represent each day of the week: at a person, that is, who reminds them why they hate or love "Tuesday" so specifically and so much. This usually gives the steps more specificity.

But working with the former problem—the "super-objective" or structure of the exercise—is the more difficult one by far, partly because "climbing a ladder," either of confrontation or exhortation, presents sizeable problems for acting students who are intellectually oriented, or emotionally restrained, or relentlessly ironic, or who generally prefer to be seen exhibiting grace under pressure rather than raw anger or rampant enthusiasm. Acting students often fall into these descriptions. There is nothing wrong, of course, with tactics of cool disdain and clever understatement, but they sorely limit the theatrical palette and diminish the dynamic intensity of human intercourse, real or fictive. Raising your voice and implying violence, or expressing unbridled enthusiasm, though entirely life-like and theatrically exciting, tend to evoke such emotional barriers as performance anxiety (stage fright) and evaluation apprehension (academic timidity). This exercise can be a comfortable way of breaking through these barriers, of encouraging students to "climb a ladder" and, scaling new emotional heights, transcend their own inhibitions and be happy they did. Escalation of feeling, publicly expressed, can be a thrilling experience for speaker and hearer alike. The exercise, simple and content-limited as it is, can be deeply moving and/or utterly hilarious. Easily translated, it can quickly bridge national and cultural barriers. I have found it internationally useful, a sturdy pedagogical tool for eliciting and guiding artistic growth.

But it cannot reach its fruition without a frank (and, I hope, illuminating) discussion of theory. The exercise stimulates consideration of theories of dramaturgy and acting: the contrasts, for example, and seeming disharmonies between objective and super-objective; the dialectic of moment-to-moment reality and structural pattern; the paradoxes of life and art. Without this sort of grounding, "I hate/love Monday" is merely a technical exercise in scale, something you "have to do" without understanding its relationship with life. Theory ennobles this pedagogical tool and persuades reluctant students to commit to its lessons and explore its implications. The teacher does not have to hammer away at his or her own authority or experience but let the exercise itself do the work. And, as always in a good exercise, the students learn more from each other than from the instructor as the work begins to take shape.

So let's go back to the initial question: why should acting students hate acting theory? Partly, of course, because they're impatient and "just" want to get the job done. Partly because they're afraid that thinking about acting may diminish their instinctual impulses (and, of course, it might). Partly, perhaps, because they've bought into the celebrity-interview line: that acting is just a matter of natural genius, or being true to oneself, or to one's nutritional or Zen guru. And partly because we, their teachers, sometimes inundate them with what to them appears as useless verbiage.

Virtually nothing I've said in these pages is intended to be shared—in its current form, anyway—with acting students. It almost certainly wouldn't interest them; nor would it necessarily help them. Practical theory, to be helpful, must come out of practical work, as wheel-wrighting theory came out of dragging carcasses to the firepit. My own pedagogical goal is always to start with the work of acting (the exercise, in this case) and allow the students themselves to evolve the theory—when it arises—out of the act of performance. This essay is directed to acting teachers: to indicate one teacher's approach to guiding that evolution, and of translating practical acting theory into a useful acting pedagogy.

WORKS CITED

Shakespeare, William. *Othello. Yale Shakespeare.* New Haven: Yale University Press, 1918.

Stanislavsky, Konstantin. *An Actor Prepares.* Trans. Elizabeth Reynolds Hapgood. New York: Theatre Arts, 1946.

CHAPTER

3 The English Secret

Just remember, there's many an actor sleeping on the embankment tonight, with no soles to his shoes, for lack of an upward inflection.
—Donald Sinden, English classical actor

For many years, American actors have lamented the fact that New York theatre audiences (and critics even more so) have reserved their greatest admiration for British actors. Just to name some recent English winners of the Broadway Tony Award: Ralph Fiennes, Maggie Smith, Janet McTeer, Diana Rigg, Nigel Hawthorne, Derek Jacobi, Jeremy Irons, Ian McKellen, Roger Rees, Constance Cummings, Jessica Tandy, Stephen Dillane, Jennifer Ehle, and Pauline Collins have all taken home the coveted New York's best actor/actress award during the past two decades. And in films, where there are no union restraints on non-national casting, British actors are not only ubiquitous, they are routinely earning high praise not only for their British and classical roles, but for playing contemporary Americans as well—with Rupert Everett, Jude Law, Kate Winslet, Ben Kingsley, Minnie Driver, Albert Finney, Ewan McGregor, Ian Holm, Patrick Stewart, Ian McKellan and Alan Rickman coming quickly to mind. Most astonishingly, Anthony Hopkins recently played President Nixon and Emma Thompson played an American First Lady, both to high acclaim.

If there's a single reason for this new British invasion, it is quite possibly the "English secret," an acting technique that, while rarely taught in America, is a routine part of English actor training. The English secret is hardly obscure, however: it's simply a mastery of the upward pitch inflection that is abundantly common in everyday speech on both sides of the Atlantic, and indeed, in virtually every language.

Originally published, in different form, in *Acting One,* fifth edition, McGraw-Hill, 2002

Pitch inflections—they can be rising or falling—are buried in the deep structures of speech; they are as essential for communication in spoken languages as punctuation and syntax are in written ones. For example, the two English sentences:

"He's going out?"
and
"He's going out!"

employ identical words in the identical order; the only difference between the two is punctuation in the written form and pitch inflection in the spoken. In spoken English (as well as spoken French, German, Spanish, et. al.), a raised inflection on the last syllable firmly indicates a question, while a falling inflection indicates a statement. But that's not all they do.

Indeed, conversation analysts have accorded pitch inflections a broad and primary sub-semantic role in all spoken communications. Willem J.M. Levelt writes, for example, "Intonation is . . . an expressive device. Pitch accent expresses the prominence of a concept, the interest adduced to it by the speaker, or its contrastive role. The melody of an utterance expresses a speaker's emotions and attitudes. It is a main device for transmitting the rhetorical force of an utterance, its weight, its obnoxiousness, its intended friendliness or hostility. It also signals the speaker's intention to continue or to halt, or to give the floor to an interlocutor."[1] And as to its ubiquity, Levelt concludes that the "relation between pitch range and intended attentional effect might well be universal in the world's languages."[2]

Inflections thus serve many practical purposes in spoken syntax besides differentiating interrogatives from declaratives.

Specifically, we use *upward* inflections (denoted in this essay by a caret [^] before the raised syllable, or multiple carets [^^ and ^^^] for an even higher pitch inflection) for several reasons, among them:

- to highlight a key word: "He plays many sports but particularly likes ^golf."

- to point out antithetical words: "Give the ball to ^^John, not ^Jim."

- to articulate a complex argument, or set of instructions: "Go ^left, then left a^^gain, then ^^^right . . ."

- to stimulate a surge of excitement: "^Show me the ^^^money!"
- to arouse enthusiasm: "Cry God for ^Harry, ^^England and ^^^Saint ^^^^George!"

- to build increasing momentum in a mere listing of nouns or adjectives: "She is my ^goods, my ^^chattels; she is my ^house, my household ^^stuff, my ^^^field, my ^^^^barn, my ^^^^^horse, my ^^^^^^ox, my ^^^^^^^ass, my ^^^^^^^^anything."

By contrast, we use *downward* inflections (denoted here by one or more downslashes[\] following the downwardly inflected syllable) basically:

- to create a sense of finality: "Our day is done.\"

- to complete an idea: "Two plus six is eight.\"

- to conclude an utterance: "I have nothing else to say.\"

In general, upward inflections create liveliness and ongoing enthusiasm, while downward inflections create decisiveness and closure. The skillful deployment of both sorts of inflections, and of the infinite possible gradations between them, transmits both in life and on the stage, qualities of infectious energy, forceful authority, and a confident, expressive persona. Moreover, as these inflections are directly drawn from everyday speech, the qualities we perceive as infectious, authoritative and expressive are also perceived as natural and lifelike. The actor who can master inflections, therefore, is likely to be seen not only as theatrically charismatic, but truthfully human, a delicious combination for the stage.

Let me briefly go over some of the basics of certain common inflections in everyday conversation—and consequently their effective use on the stage.

ASKING — OR NOT ASKING — QUESTIONS

The rising inflection at the end of questions—particularly for questions one genuinely wishes to be answered—has some important acting implications.

The upward inflection at the end of these questions (which can also come on the penultimate syllable):

Are you ^sure?

Did you ^win?

Are you going to the ^game?

Did you ^like ^^it? (or sometimes ^^like ^it?)

specifically *engages* the person addressed; by actively soliciting an answer (even if one never comes), the inflection makes the question interactional. It is a sort of hook that draws the asker to the askee, and even a momentary pause following such an inflection is normally pregnant with situational possibilities creating, on stage, genuine suspense. By powerfully engaging both actors, the one asking and the one asked, and by creating a dynamic interaction (instead of a mere exchange of information) between them, such a question also engages the audience.

Not all questions genuinely solicit answers, however. Some apparent questions are in fact implicit criticisms—normally denoted by a falling inflection:

Are you sure\ (as if to add "you idiot!")

Are you going to the game\ (as if to add "instead of to my party?")

The downwardly inflected question seeks to confer humiliation rather than solicit a response; instead of hooking the askee, it figuratively looks down one's nose. Compared to its upwardly inflected counterpart, it is less interactional, and therefore less inducive of suspense or dynamic momentum. Actors unduly prone to such inflections may be trying to project an attitude—but they generally rob their own performances of interactive vibrancy and magnetism.

POINTING ANTITHESES

Upward inflections are crucial in indicating both parts of an antithesis, with the preferred alternative getting a higher inflection than its counterpart:

Not ^left, but ^^right.

It's ^^right, not ^left.

Notice that the preferred word ("right" in this case) is inflected further upward regardless of which position—first or second—it has in the sentence. Similarly:

I like ^^June, not ^May.
^May is fine, but ^^June's divine!

That inflections are crucial for communication becomes even more evident when we pose antitheses to children, or persons with less-developed intellectual skills:

Don't ride your bike in the ^street, ride on the ^^^^sidewalk!
Ride your bike on the ^^^^sidewalk, not in the ^street.

Antitheses, of course, are the stuff of logic, the push and pull of argumentation; by defining both sides of a dialectic, antitheses make the general specific. Shakespeare, of course, depended heavily on them ("It's ^^Helena, not ^Hermia I love" "Give every man thy ^^ear, but few thy ^voice"), but so do all dramatists whose characters believe they have something important to say.

KEY WORDS: IMPLIED ANTITHESES

Key or "operative" words generally indicate implied antitheses, with the antithetical term understood but unstated. They too are usually highlighted by an upward inflection:

Ann's going to Phila^delphia tomorrow. (instead of to Chicago)

Ann's going to Philadelphia to^morrow. (instead of the day after tomorrow)

^Ann's going to Philadelphia tomorrow. (instead of Jane going there)

Ann's ^going to Philadelphia tomorrow. (instead of coming back from there)

Notice that if this were simply a statement of fact, and did not contradict any previous assumption (as "Ann's going to Chicago tomorrow") it would, in normal conversation, be largely uninflected. One reason you rarely find simple statements of fact in dramatic works is that they create neither suspense nor momentum.

Implied and often complex antitheses lurk everywhere in logical speech. As in Horatio's urging to the Ghost:

If there be any good thing to be done,
That may to thee do ease and grace to me . . .

As *good* is antithetical to the implied (but unstated) *bad,* it would ordinarily be given a lifted pitch accent. And as thee and me are, if not precisely antithetical, then at least two sides of a spirit/human equation, they too would, for greatest clarity, be pointed by upward inflections. The urging becomes a more strongly articulated inter-action when Horatio says:

If there be any ^good thing to be done,
That may to ^^thee do ease | and grace to ^^^me . . .

A millisecond pause[3] after "ease," here indicated by a vertical line [|], further articulates the different presumed desires of the Ghost (physical comfort, relief of purgatorial suffering) versus those of Horatio (spiritual fulfillment, state of divine knowledge). A mastery of the inflections in this passage can then touch on subtle but profound meanings that at first seem tangential to the core goal or objective ("Speak to me!" which follows immediately) of the speech.

MOMENTUM

And finally, upward inflections provide, in our daily conversation as well as on stage, a powerful momentum, carrying the central idea of a sentence through its natural speaking and breathing pauses (usually marked in the written text by commas) that separate clauses, phrases, or separate items on a list. Thus:

^Well, I went to the ^store that your mother told me ab^out, and bought some ^grapes, some as^^parag^us, some ^^^peas, some ^^^^cauliflow^er, a ^^^^^news-pap^er, and some ^freshly ^baked ^^^^^^bread\\.

(Normally, the pitch on "bread" would start very high, as the apex of the list, and then slide down the scale by word's end.)

On stage, this momentum is quite simply what makes drama dramatic. And momentous.

Returning to Horatio's speech to the Ghost, we can see that a series of rising and falling inflections create, not only an appealing musicality (which Horatio might feel particularly suitable for invoking a spirit), but the articulation of an *escalating* appeal to a reluctant responder.

^Stay, illusion\!

If thou hast any ^sound, or ^use of ^^voice,
^^^Speak to me.\

If there be any ^^good thing to be done,
That may to ^^thee do ease and grace to ^^^me,
^^^^Speak to me!\\

If thou art ^^^privy to thy country's ^^^fate,
Which happily fore^^^^knowing may av^^^^oid,
^^^^^O^^^^^^^speak!

That this should be an escalating appeal is a situational necessity: Horatio doesn't actually want to make three requests, he would be most happy if the Ghost would answer him on the first "Speak to me." But the Ghost doesn't—and Horatio has to try again. And try harder. This "build" is not merely an escalation of pitches, of course, it is a build in intensity, in desire, in emotion; it is an escalation of the fear that the "country's fate" is in peril, and in the fervent hope that foreknowledge—and consequent action—can save the nation. It is, in other words, captivating drama, and it captures not merely the audience's attention, but their sympathy and participation.

Pitch changes here are a mini-concerto of in-line and between-line builds. The slight intralinear pitch build from *sound* to *use of voice* dramatizes Horatio's growing hope that while it would be wonderful if the Ghost could make sound, it would be far better if he could actually speak. The more multifaceted interlinear builds from "Stay" to "Speak" to a second "Speak" to a final "O speak!", showing that Horatio is trying harder with each request. Similarly the interlinear build from "use of voice" to "good thing" to "privy" to "fate" to "foreknowing" and "avoid" accelerates those arguments with which Horatio supports his request.

SO WHY IS LEARNING THIS SO HARD?

Making these everyday inflections part of everyday acting is, however, a tougher task than one might expect. One might reasonably ask that, if inflections are simply a part of ordinary speaking, why must actors be taught to make them? Why don't they just do this naturally?

Well, they do, *but only if they are fully committed to pursuing their character's goal with the other people onstage.*

Let's make no mistake about it: actors who are truly "experiencing" their roles onstage, as Stanislavsky proposed,[4] will be speaking from their character's mind (or heart) as well as through their character's mouth, and their inflections will always be natural. And therefore perfect.

But that's much easier said than done. For the fact is that actors normally must speak words they don't themselves think up, but have in fact memorized out of a book written by someone else.

Moreover, they often speak in accents or linguistic styles (verse, for example) that don't come naturally to them in their daily lives.

It is therefore inescapable that in many cases actors—including veteran professionals—will find themselves, at least in early rehearsals, essentially reciting memorized lines rather than speaking words derived solely from their character's situation. For the fact is that acting a scripted and memorized role is a fundamentally unnatural way to initiate speech. And unnatural inflections often result. And worse, through constant repetition in rehearsals, these unnatural (and decidedly non-interactive and undramatic) inflections often find their way into actual productions.

As an example of recitational inflections, consider the first words of the pledge of allegiance recited by schoolchildren throughout the United States:

> I pledge allegiance\
> To the flag\
> of the United\ States\ of America\\ . . .

The inflections fall (one might say "die") because they are not addressed to anyone, and they are not uttered in response to any situation. As an exercise makes clear,[5] when someone truly imagines a situation from which such an utterance could logically derive (as someone actually pledging his allegiance to the flag of an adopted new country, in his own words, at the moment he first sets eyes on it), the inflections would be more like:

I pledge al^legiance
To the ^^flag
Of the United States of Am^^^erica!\

Thus in order to make the shift from unnatural to natural (and thereby dramatic) inflecting, actors must learn to make the transition from reciting memorized texts—whether the pledge of allegiance or the part of Hedda Gabler—to speaking such texts as though the words had sprung spontaneously from their own minds, and for the purpose of winning their characters' goals. Whether to address this directly, by calling attention to inflections and such "technical" aspects of vocal delivery, or indirectly, simply by working on the goals and tactics of each character, remains an open question, but I think it is useful to proceed with the tentative answer of "some of each," depending, certainly, on the text and persons (and time) involved. And, in any case, the subject should certainly be addressed, or at least discussed, during any period of serious actor training.

INFLECTIONS AND ACTOR TRAINING

The actor's use of pitch inflections has been discussed—at least in England—for at least two and a half centuries. As early as 1750, the Englishman John Hill wrote of "monotonous actors" who have "too frequent repetitions of the same inflections. When they have blank verse put into their mouths, [they] . . . seem to think it a duty to close every sentence an octave below."[6]

But we shouldn't relegate Hill's remarks on inflections merely to a purely external acting technique; Hill was actually an early advocate of "natural" acting (the actor "must feel every thing strongly that he would have his audience feel."[7]). And Konstantin Stanislavsky, the patron saint of "internal" acting, spoke eloquently about the external importance of inflections to produce not just clarity but also feelings:

The external word, by means of intonation, affects one's emotion, memory, feelings . . . Intonations and pauses, in themselves, possess the power to produce a powerful emotional effect on the listener.[8]

Just what did Stanislavsky mean by intonation? It was his term (or rather his translator's term) for an "upward twist to the sound of the last syllable." He particularly prized the upward inflection for its ability to create suspense and sustain an idea through a breathing pause:

Give an upward twist to the sound of the last syllable of the last word before the comma . . . [and] leave the high note hanging in the air for a bit . . . Almost like the warning lift of a hand, [it] causes listeners to wait patiently for the end of the unfinished sentence. Do you realize how important this is? [It provides] the satisfaction of lifting your phonetic line before a comma and waiting confidently, because you know surely that no one will interrupt or hurry you."[9]

Stanislavsky made clear that this was not merely a single upward twist, but a complex scoring of syllables, which he could only describe in musical terms: "This rising melodic line can take on all kinds of twists and go to all kinds of heights: in intervals of thirds, fifths, octaves, with a short steep rise, or a broad, smooth, small swing and so on."[10] To an actor who, while storming through Othello's great "Pontic Sea" speech, did not know how to build his argument, Stanislavsky advised, "Not so flat . . . put some design in! . . . See that the second measure is stronger than the first, the third stronger than the second, the fourth than the third. But no shouting! Noise is not power! Power lies in heightening."[11] To an actor who was merely shouting, Stanislavsky leveled a particularly trenchant attack: "Don't you know that the power lies in the logic, the coherence of what you are saying? And you destroy it. When you need power, pattern your voice and your inflections in a varied phonetic line, from top to bottom. When you need real power in your speech, forget about volume, and remember your rising and falling inflections."[12]

But in our time, it has been not the Russians, and certainly not the Americans, but the English who have taken the lead on this matter. Cicely Berry, the distinguished long-time voice coach for the Royal Shakespeare Company, is a major advocate: "Where there is a break within the line . . . [usually] it is simply a poise on a word—i.e., the word holds and lifts for a fraction of a moment before it plunges into the second half of the line. This poise is necessary for the ear of the listener in that it allows a space, a still moment, for us to clock the key word in the line, and so be ready for the information in the second half of the line . . . Very often, when we do not understand a speech, it is because this shaping has not been attended to."[13]

English director Michael Langham, formerly artistic director of the Guthrie Theatre and the Stratford (Ontario) Shakespeare Festival, waxes more poetical but to the same end: "If we take a downward inflection, we finish the journey. Keep the journey going, keep the inflection buoyantly up, until we reach the end of the trip."[14]

None of this was ever mentioned—much less discussed and/or taught—during my studies at the Yale Drama School in the 60s, nor by Lee Strasberg when I attended the Actors Studio in the same period, nor was the subject brought up in the major American acting books of the 60s and 70s—certainly not by Hagen, Benedetti, or McGaw.[15] Nor did I broach the subject in my first acting book (*Acting Power*) of 1978. Indeed, it would take a brave American in the heyday of the Actors Studio— the 50s, 60s, or 70s—to even mention such seemingly technical aspects of acting performance as inflections and vocal pitch, which were addressed, if at all, by directors giving line readings to actors (e.g., "No, Janet, it's not 'wherefore ^art thou, Romeo,' it's 'wherefore art thou ^^Romeo'"!)

And so I first learned about the importance of pitch inflections from a British actor: Brewster Mason, a veteran of the Royal Shakespeare Company who spent several of his last years teaching on my campus during the early 1970s. "American actors don't know how to give the *feed*!" Brewster would complain to me, referring specifically to that upward inflection at the end of a line that sets up a cue in such a way that the actor who speaks the next line can knock it out of the park. I, and most of my American colleagues, considered Mason's complaint absurdly old-fashioned at the time; even demeaning: as if the actor's goal was really to be a restaurant waiter. But I've changed my views: "Feeding" your acting partner with charged, upwardly-inflecting cues ("Are you going ^^out?), and being aggressively fed by your partner in return, creates drama that is powerfully interactive. I'm not always sure whether this is best addressed from the inside (by helping the actor live the part fully) or from the outside ("try lifting that last syllable a bit, OK?"), but it's clear to me that an actor's awareness of inflections in life, and their importance in creating the dynamics and momentum of a great stage production, leads to enhanced performances wherever the process originates.

Mastery of inflections is not the most important skill an actor must employ, of course. It's probably not even in the top ten. But in a field as competitive as professional stage acting, where only one in a thousand succeed, and only one in a thousand of those (rising inflection there too!) will succeed sufficiently to have a lifetime career, the extra margin of excellence will make all the difference. At minimum, an awareness of the nature of inflections in normal conversation can key a director or coach as to when an actor is not fully experiencing (or thinking) the part, and what work needs be done to correct this. At maximum, inflectional mastery can help an actor deliver five things absolutely crucial for professional success: clear articulation of ideas, dramatic momentum and suspense, excitement and charisma, brimming confidence, and (yes!) believability.

For that's the only secret of the English secret: Inflecting is Believing.

NOTES

1 *Speaking: From Intention to Articulation,* MIT Press: 1989), p. 307.

2 Ibid, pp. 316/17.

3 Technically a *caesura* here, since this is a verse line.

4 *Perezhivanie,* often translated as "living the part." See Carnicke, *Stanislavsky in Focus;* Amsterdam: Harwood Academic Publishers, 1998.

5 See the video, *Acting One: Day One with Robert Cohen,* Mayfield Publishing Company, 1998, or, for a written description, my *Acting One,* Fourth edition, McGraw Hill, 2001.

6 *The Actor, A Treatise on the Art of Playing,* London: R. Griffiths, pp. 199, 198.

7 Ibid, p. 106.

8 Ibid, p. 132, 137.

9 *Building a Character.*

10 Ibid, p. 126.

11 Ibid, pp. 160-61.

12 Ibid, p. 138.

13 Cicely Berry, *Voice and the Actor,* London, Harrap, 1973.

14 *Journal for Stage Directors and Choreographers*, Spring/Summer 2000, p. 10.

15 Uta Hagen (*Respect For Acting*, Macmillan 1973) correctly argues against "delivering the words mechanically with set, intellectualized intonations" (p. 71) and advises that to "memorize the words and mechanize the inflections" in advance of rehearsals "can be fatal," but she never otherwise addresses how non-mechanically approached inflections can prove useful. Robert L. Benedetti (*The Actor At Work*, Third edition, Prentice-Hall, 1981) discusses the actor's use of "vocal melody" as a "physical manifestation of appropriate connotations," (pp. 160-61) and says that "when we fully revitalize the melody of a speech, we find that the sounds help to make the feelings and meaning more vivid and immediate," (p. 163) and that "structural figures" such as antitheses demand "the utmost skill from the actor in the use of inflection, emphasis, pitch, and supportive gesture," but doesn't go into what these inflections or pitches might be. In early editions, Charles McGaw (*Acting Is Believing,* Rinehart & Company, 1955), says little more than "the basis for effective interpretation of lines is a good voice," (Second edition, p.96); in later editions he added a chapter on "Speaking the Lines" which discussed emphasizing "operative words" (Fifth edition, 1986, p. 198)

and, paraphrasing Grotowski, "keeping the sentence moving towards its epicentrum," but, like the others, does not specifically discuss how pitch inflection achieves this.

CHAPTER

4 Intro/Extrospective Analysis

A study of Acting takes place in at least two thousand American colleges and universities these days, and is in fact a core curriculum in at least several hundred American graduate programs. And yet the pedagogical methods that come into play in this field, particularly in the U.S., often represent remarkable departures from most instructional strategies.

Paramount among these is a rather surprising concentration on the student's own self-evaluation of his or her work and progress. Moreover, this is not only an evaluation of the achieved level of performance; it is often an introspectively-derived report (and apparent measurement) of the "feelings" the student reports experiencing during or following that performance. It is common, for example, for an acting instructor to initiate a post-performance critique by asking the student-actors, "How did you feel about your scene?" This can be, in fact, a double question (although this is not always recognized); its separate and quite distinct inquiries being: "How do you feel the scene went?" (e.g., successfully, poorly) and "What emotions did you experience while performing?" (e.g., sad, exhilarated). Quite often the students' responses to this question will then frame, if not center, the entire ensuing discussion.

Parallels in other disciplines are hard to come by: it would be virtually unthinkable, for example, for an instructor in dental school to devote substantial class time to how a student dentist "felt" while performing a root canal. And pedagogies in most (if not all) other professional disciplines—such as law, plumbing, accounting, architecture, viniculture, etc.—are strictly focused on (if not limited to) teaching demonstrable mastery of, and possible alternatives to, accepted professional technique, as taught, evaluated, and certified by recognized masters of that technique, with student self-evaluation playing little or no role in this process.

Originally published, in different form, in *The Beat*, Winter 1993

Much of the privileging of self-evaluation (and self-emotional evaluation) comes from the rebellion, starting in the last years of the previous century, against "conserve-toire" training, which emphasized precise technical modelling by accomplished doyens, or old masters. This is often ridiculed as "result" training, which, in the post-war period of arts instruction, is usually considered subsidiary to "process" training.

Much, of course, comes from the influence of Stanislavsky, and, in this country, from Lee Strasberg's variation of the early Stanislavsky teaching.

"Early" in this case means acting that is emotion-centered, as opposed to action-centered. Lee Strasberg expanded this early Stanislavsky notion so as to privilege the actor's own personality in a way that even the early Stanislavsky would have thought bizarre. Strasberg begins with a relatively secure Stanislavskyan base, as he speaks of "the central problem of the actor: How can the actor both really feel, and also be in control of what he needs to do on stage . . . " Not only is this grounded in Stanislavsky, it is grounded in David Garrick and earlier writers as well. However, Strasberg then moved to "a second problem: How can the actor make his real feelings expressive on the stage?" (*A Dream of Passion,* 6). This apparently simple idea contains an element of true revolution: the "problem" of acting is not so much the playing of a character, but the expressing your own "real" feelings.

This begins a theatre of self-therapy, of "private moments" where actors were encouraged to indulge in their emotional memories and exploit them in class (and presumably onstage). Strasberg's Studio therefore attracted, in addition to highly ego-centric movie stars like Brando and Dean, highly disturbed (and reality-seeking) actors like Monroe and Winters, who seemed eager to make art (or at least something) out of their lives.

Of course, there is a clear pedagogical basis for at least some self-evaluation. Acting is an art, and surely has a more subjective base than, say, dentistry. It's also less dangerous: a bad performance is only rarely as painful as a botched root canal. And character emotion—perceived character emotion, anyway—is certainly one of the basic languages of the stage. The overwhelming tradition of acting theory, Diderot aside, has therefore been to encourage a blending (if not a superimposition) of "real" actor-emotion onto "perceived" character emotion, thus making the actor's putative "real" feelings part and parcel of the role played. This is true at least since Plato's *Ion,* and Horace's dictum (you only move the audience by being moved yourself), and carries through John Hill, Sainte Albine, David Garrick, and of course Stanislavsky and his followers.

It has even been extended—first by Brecht and subsequently by performance artists, postmodernists, and cultural pluralists into a broader socially and culturally based self evaluation, where the actor is encouraged to superpose his/her ethnic/social identity onto the character's, thus expanding the egocentric perspective to an entho-centric one. This, too, marginalizes or excludes the outside evaluator: "you wouldn't understand, it's a guy thing." Or "a black thing."

Yet the fact that demonstrable (expert-evaluated) mastery of technique is, in certain actor-training classes, on a secondary footing with a student's self-evaluation (particularly of his or her own fluctuating emotional state) poses pronounced pedagogical dilemmas. What is the role of the instructor? Is introspection a satisfactory educational process? Is self-evaluation a primary artistic criterion? Where does self-evaluation fit into a determination of craft mastery?

Before addressing these dilemmas, I'd like to open another, even broader issue, which is the complex and often bewildering relations between competing definitions of "acting": as a behavior, as an art, as a career, and as an identity.

These are not merely semantic confusions: the simple statement, "I am an actor," is fraught with fundamental psychological and even ontological implications, which are both perplexing on the philosophical level, and quite maddening—sometimes even pathogenic—on the personal. The well-known pragmatic realities of acting as a career focus this issue sharply: Given the extremely high unemployment rate in the acting profession, and the statistical fact that less than 10% of those persons enrolled in professional actor-training programs will ever develop anything resembling an extended professional acting career, acting students experience levels of anxiety and insecurity quite beyond those of persons training for more accessible professions.

The confluence of this issue with the prior one presents a true crux: since the "real" world so rarely confers professional status and identity (by way of steady union employment), the graduating student is more likely to seek ontological security through his or her self-evaluation as an actor-artist. And the self-evaluation, now lacking an entourage of experts/masters (teachers) or a critical audience (classmates), becomes more and more a self-absorption: an analysis of one's own feelings. "I would kill for this role," a common thespian wisecrack, often springs from a deeply buried, if unconscious, despair.

And on top of even these dilemmas is our overarching problem in evaluating acting pedagogies themselves; a problem stemming from the fact that successful career actors, who presumably could look back over their prior training and advise us on the relative merits of various pedagogical techniques, are, at best, publicly forgetful of the teachings that brought them to eminence. "I was a terrible student" is the refrain we see on all the talk shows, where actors regularly appear to trumpet their natural, untaught genius. "My teachers said I would never make it," and "They all urged me to go into bookkeeping" is about all we hear from our superstars today, who boast about their struggles as waiters, boxers, and taxidrivers, never as acting class students at University State. And where the occasional acting instructor is mentioned, it is usually a guru who persuaded the supernova "just to be honest," or "just to be myself"—as distinct from those other teachers who were, presumably, trying to make him or her affected and hypocritical. Thus, acting instructors often become self-evaluators too, as they lack an articulate and objective cohort of progeny (graduates) who could provide the necessary data on what it actually takes to develop professional excellence in the acting art.

These problems, as averred above, cohere; one feeds the other. The actor's wish to appear as naturally gifted, rather than as technically trained, feeds his/her wish to believe that acting is an identity rather than an art or craft. A reliance on introspective rather than external evaluation, which is then based on felt emotion rather than demonstrable mastery, isolates the acting student from teacher and fellow student alike, suggesting that the superstar is alienated from his or her own developmental process. This alienation often becomes reified as part of a "star mystique;" it is difficult to imagine, for example, Robin Williams or Kevin Kline working his way through the International Phonetic Alphabet or to physically climax rhetorical cadenzas—but they did!

And this mystique of acting clouds, as it is supposed to do, considerations of prior training and effective pedagogy.

I would be happy to provide solutions to all these problems, but I am little better at it than 2,000 years of theorists; the solution ultimately must be based on the secret alloy of Dionysian ecstasy and Apollonian objectivity that Nietzsche and others have labored, almost uselessly, to identify.

All I can say at this point is that we must keep the dialectic alive, and not simplify the issue gracelessly by opting for either a sterile objectivity nor a capitulation to solepsicistic self-referentiality.

We probably need an effective extrinsic taxonomy of evaluative terms. Something more than the checklist one finds in URTA applications or the recommendation forms of Shakespeare festivals. Terms that deal with the dynamics and excitement and even the mystique of theatre itself.

Towards such terms I do have some suggestions. Let's aim for acting achievements that:

- develop momentum
- create suspense and anticipation
- engage feelings and empathy
- excite emotion
- convey a story
- demand attention
- provoke reflection
- infect and move fellow actors
- surprise, shock, alarm, amaze, and absorb the spectator.

Is work aimed at this taxonomy just another form of "result" training? I suppose it is. But the dichotomy between process and result has, I fear, been mislabelled. A "process" only becomes a process when it is directed towards a result.

Otherwise it is simply a random set of actions and behaviors. Process is, by definition, not random, and it is not omnidirectional. Ideally, neither process nor result should ever be seen in isolation, and the effectiveness of any acting pedagogy, or analysis, is, in the long run, proportional to the ability to keep both the process and the result in equal (and conjoint) focus.

CHAPTER

5

Answers to Questions

I wish to make a short report on a theatrical project, recently completed, that could point the way to a new dramatic/theatrical genre of high potential. The genre might be called "documentary drama." It consists, in brief, of actors playing a text that has been transcribed verbatim from real-life dialog occurring among persons whose identities are to remain unknown—to actors and audience alike. The potential of this genre is extraordinary for both audience interest and actor development.

The project took the form of a 25-minute theatre piece entitled *Answers To Questions I*, conceived and created by Marilyn Mooney and myself, and performed on the stage in the winter of 1975 at the University of California, Irvine. It has subsequently been made into a film entitled "Inside Looking In (and Sometimes Out)" under the sponsorship of the American Personnel and Guidance Association of Washington, D.C., and has been distributed nationally.

Answers To Questions I consists specifically of 15 student-actors assembling on stage and directly addressing to the audience a section of 100 speeches drawn from a series of anonymous interview transcripts. The solicitation and collection of these transcripts comprised the first phase of the project, in which Mooney, during the autumn of 1974, randomly selected passersby at a campus dining hall. These students were informed of the nature of our project, and agreed to answer personal questions posed by Mooney and have their responses tape recorded: The questions were as simple and unstructured as possible: How do you spend your day? What do you like to do? Who do you think you are? What do you think about death? What do you want out of life? Names were neither asked nor given. The tape recording was then transcribed into a typescript, and the tape was erased—the student-interviewee's identity was now irretrievable. At that point the project went into its second, or editing, phase. The intact transcripts were next given to student actors at the same University

Originally published in *The Drama Review*, Fall 1975

campus—one transcript to each actor. (The transcripts were randomly assigned, except when it was obvious that an interviewee was of a certain sex; then the transcript was given to an actor of like sex.) The actors were asked to study and edit the transcripts into appropriate narrative statements. These statements could be as short as a sentence or as long as two pages, and the actors were asked to edit as many statements as they felt were of interest as revelations of character. The editing in all cases retained the verbatim responses to the questions, and the context of the interview situation, with the exception of occasional syntactical rewording where absolutely necessary. After the edited statements were given to Mooney and myself, we further edited them down and compiled them into an arrangement of 100 statements to be delivered in a seemingly random order. In the final phase of the project, the actors committed "their" statements to memory, learned their cues, took positions on a stage (bare of scenery, but with rehearsal furniture), and "performed" the 100 statements of their fellow students by speaking them directly to the audience.

The random order of the statements was, of course, greatly influenced by my and Mooney's theatrical instincts. Some of the sequencing took the form of short, pithy comments followed by a rambling speech tending to sum them up. One character revealed himself in seventeen epigrammatic (and contradictory) statements spaced equally throughout the production, while another was edited into a single disjunctive monologue which went pathetically around in inconclusive circles. This character was the only one given movement—she ambled forward as she spoke, and retired to her chair after she was finished. Some of the sequencing had an ironic aspect. One character repeated one of her speeches three times during the production. But nothing was done to create any particular storytelling or cathartic effect.

What was the result? The text, of course, was totally non-literary; subject only to the shapings of individual interviewees and actor/editors. The speeches, as a result, were generally inarticulate, and unlike the dialog of a Stanley Kowalski, the *Answers To Questions I* dialogue was *unintentionally* inarticulate. There was no intermediary playwright "speaking down" through his characters or roughening up his dialogue for atmosphere or "characterization." Rather, the inarticulateness came directly from conflict and struggle: the interviewee's own conflict between the hopes he tried to articulate and the reality he knew the interviewer saw. The transcripts portrayed a genuine struggle, and frequently a genuine failure: more than in conventional scripted drama, the documentary drama records precisely the difference between intention and accomplishment, and it does so in the case of persons quite like ourselves. What we have in the dialog, and what we see abundantly, is an unvarnished struggle for personal expression: not in grand themes, intriguing plots, or outlandish characters, but in the ongoing, moment-to-moment process of speaking and being heard. We see very clearly the thoughts between the lines, and we know that they are *real* thoughts, really thought, and not the fabrications of a playwright. For example:

> I think that everybody should be able to explore different levels of consciousness and awareness. You know. Planes of experience. So, you know, I like to see what's happening as much as possible. I like to sit around with my friends. Get loaded. I don't have a lot of friends. I usually sit around and get loaded by myself.

I am not going to argue that this transcribed statement is spontaneous in the purest sense. Obviously it was influenced, during the interview, by the presence of the interviewer, and it was probably influenced by the interviewee's fantasy of a larger (theatre) audience who would eventually hear his statement. This does not detract from the reality of the statement, however; probably all of our discourse, and perhaps even our private thinking, is affected by the real or imaginary audiences which we carry around in the backs of our heads. What I am saying is that the thinking which we see between lines here *really happened* in the interview. As we see the speaker's recognition which leads him to say "I don't have a whole lot of friends," we also realize that this recognition occurred at the same moment in the interview. Any Aristotelian will see that this speech contains the classic dramaturgical features of *anagnorisis* (recognition) and *peripeteia* (reversal), but here we realize that the dramaturgical features were not put in by any playwright. If we are being manipulated, it is by the actor/character, not by the playwright/director, and we cannot help but be intrigued and compassionate. We have not been "set up"; the dramaturgical punch of the speech is organic, not artificial.

What of the actor? Again, there can be no statement that the actor is somehow magically spontaneous in documentary drama; however he *is* in somewhat of an extraordinary position. In the first place, he has no indication of his "character" outside of what he says. There is absolutely no information derived externally; there is no plot, there is no known future, and there is only an inferred past. Moreover, there is no model to achieve or stand up to or defend oneself against: the role has no history, has never been played before, and cannot be challenged for accuracy by anyone. This brings the actor to a first level of freedom.

In directing the piece, I insisted that the actor *in no way try to characterize their roles*, but that instead they perform their parts in their own voices, in their own clothing, and with their own earnestness. I further instructed them to present the best possible case for their character, to develop the same epistemological egocentricity as the character has (and as all people have), and to assume that they were the hero of their own play-within-a-play. To emphasize this further (for it is a difficult concept to experience, if not to understand), I suggested that if a friend of the actor were to walk in and hear the actor saying these words, and if the words were markedly "out-of-character" for the actor himself, that the friend would have to decide that there were things about the actor that he hadn't known—rather than realize that he was witnessing the actor rehearse a memorized part authored by someone else.

This brings the actor to a second level of freedom. For while the original interviewee is given the freedom of an anonymous identity, and can thereby say anything he feels, the actor is given the freedom of an anonymous personality, and can feel anything he says. When the actor says the line, for example,

Well, when I was about thirteen, I tried to commit suicide because
I was, I felt that the whole world was so icky. And then as l grew older
I realized that the reason the whole world seemed so icky to me was
that I was just not that much of a person.

the actor can re-experience feelings to which he rarely if ever gives public voice and can make use of a vocabulary which, although primitive, has emotional referents that his more sophisticated public language cannot touch. That is, both the actor and the interviewee have the freedom of complete social irresponsibility; neither can be held personally accountable for being peurile or sentimental, and both can draw upon those wellsprings of peurility and sentimentality which, frankly, lie more at the heart of cathartic experiences than most of us like to admit. The interposition of the "shield" of anonymity, in any event, can be used to liberate deeply felt longings in interviewee, actor, and audience member alike, and the obvious objectivity of the documentary structure can free the actor from concerns of emotional over-indulgence or sentimentalizing.

The essence of documentary-drama acting is role assumption, and this is one reason why the genre is so useful in actor-training situations. I have always felt that beginning actors have a tendency to refuse identification with the role they play: a protective tendency which seeks to convey information on the order of "don't think for a moment, folks, that this could be ME you're seeing up here." So we get student Romeos who hold up, as it were, a banner that says "I, unlike Romeo who I am playing, am a cool, composed lover; this is not the way *I* would behave if *I* were in his situation." Needless to say, this tendency is detrimental to acting development, but it stems from psychological needs which are elusive and difficult to redirect. This tendency to disassociate with the role is particularly crucial in documentary drama, because the actors are asked to "play" characters who are too close for comfort—characters with whom they could, in most cases, easily be confused. Moreover, they are not allowed to "characterize" these characters. Given that we are dealing with a group of young people (college students) who are in the process of attempting to define and distinguish their own personalities for the first time in their lives, the possibility of confusing identity with a fellow-student's is particularly threatening. But precisely because the problem is exacerbated in this way, it is "put on the table" for the first time and can be confronted head-on.

I have said that our approach was to prevent the actors from characterizing their roles, and perhaps that could be put in positive terms at this point. For a long time I have felt that most of what is called character acting is not character acting at all, but only a form of character assassination. I believe the reason why this should be so is this: we (all people) inherently think of ourselves as perfect, and superior to other people. Of course we are aware that the world does not see us that way, and we have so adjusted to the world's view of us that we have filled our minds' workings with this "adjusted" reality; still, whether we be atheists or true believers, we KNOW that by the Abstract Standard Of Perfection Which Ultimately Judges Behavior, we (secretly) are ideal and superior. That this is not a rational position in no way discredits it, for it is quite universally, and quite tenaciously carried to our graves. It is the heart of the epistemological egocentrism I mentioned earlier. Well, what of it? Because we think ourselves as essentially perfect and superior, and because we think of "characterizing" details as those behaviors which differ from our own, we therefore think of "characters" as imperfect and inferior to ourselves. So that *the job of "characterizing" often becomes an exercise in worsening ourselves in order to become somebody else.* And this becomes very obvious in a documentary drama situation, when the actor's first efforts are little more than snide put-downs of the characters they play.

But as I say, this is an ideal experience to confront this role-disassociation via "characterizing." The directorial effort is to demand of the actors the very *best* possible person they could represent/create. They were to assume the character's egocentricity and sense of moral superiority. They were to assume their character's positive intentions and fantasies. They were to assume their character's struggle for happiness and lucidity. They were to represent, as it were, their character in open court, and come out a winner. If they were to fail to win, that would be the script's doing, and not their own—in any event, the audience, not the actor, determines winners and losers according to their standards. By this process the character becomes subsumed by the actor, the actor makes the fullest use of himself, and the character's original and independent identity simply disappears.

How does this all go over? Audience response to the initial *Answers To Questions I* was, as with anything staged, impossible to quantify exactly, but I must open myself to charges of immodesty by declaring that it was favorable, on three different levels. As a theatre performance, pure and simple, it was entertaining and stimulating. It was much funnier than any of us had anticipated (even discounting the usual unexpected laughs that one, after a number of years, forces oneself to expect), and it was emotionally moving in its more psychological realizations. On a second level it was highly informative as a psychosociological document, in some ways a "realer" revelation of what a certain group of individuals may be thinking than any other format. I say this for the following reason: in a true "group therapy" session, which might at first glance be thought to get closer to the heart of individuals' deepest concerns, there is a great deal of doctor-patient gameplaying which affects everything said and done. The psychic rewards for confession in therapy session are frequently so overwhelming as to induce an orgy of contrived confession, much as the priest's chamber did during Inquisition days. The intervention of an actor between the confessor and his confession, far from taking the confession a step away from reality, may in fact bring it a step closer. It was, no doubt, this second level of success which induced the American Personnel and Guidance Association to invest a large sum of money to film the production.

The third level of success was for the actors and director, who had a chance to work with undramatized material directly, and to fashion a piece of theatre out of it. I would not wish to overlook the tremendously interesting and valuable task of editing the transcripts, which was accomplished primarily by the actors themselves. Looking for the first time at undramatized narrative material as a theatrical text, the actors found subtext, motivation, intention, inner monologue, and inter-line transitional thinking in ordinary conversation; it was useful to them in examining, then, both the structure of real-life dialogue and the reality of stage action, and how the two are, or could be, related.

I can even hypothesize a fourth level of agreeable results, and that was with the interviewees. While the procedures of our work prevented me from ever meeting them, Mooney reported that virtually all were stimulated far more than any of us anticipated by the interview session, and most explained, in one way or another, that they were thrilled to be asked questions that touched their most private thoughts and meditations. Many were probably speaking to that Abstract Standard Of Perfection to whom we all, in one way or another, pay our homage. All of them were invited to the production, and some probably had the unsettling experience of hearing their own words from another's mouth. Their comments, unfortunately unsolicitable, would be of interest, I am sure.

I am aware of three instances of theatrical presentation which have some similarity to *Answers To Questions*, and might become part of the background of a developing genre of documentary drama. The first to come to my attention was a theatrical piece entitled *The Concept*, which played off-Broadway in the late 1960s, and which consisted for the most part of residents at Daytop, a half-way house for former heroin addicts, re-enacting several of their group therapy sessions. The production had a tremendously powerful effect on me and on many of those who saw it: the actors played themselves, and the entire presentation was loosely put together by a professional director out of remembered and revitalized events at the House. A second presentation format which bears discussing is the variety of staged readings of the Nixon transcripts which occurred shortly after their publication in 1974. Here, of course, the anonymity essential for *Answers to Questions* does not pertain, and I believe the temptation to characterize Nixon, Mitchell, Dean, et al, has so far proven irresistible. If the actors don't do it, the audience will. And the third example is the Broadway musical *A Chorus Line* whose text was written by Michael Bennett, Nicholas Dante, and James Kirkwood, chiefly from genuine and verbatim conversations with chorus dancers. This musical, which has enjoyed enormous success, perhaps indicates most directly the potential of the genre.

Why the potential? Because documentary drama uncovers what people are really thinking. It is voyeuristic drama at its best and least affected. It capitalizes on our profoundest curiosities without making us feel dirty; people DO want to talk, and people DO want to hear what people are thinking, but social structures and pressures have, in our times particularly, prevented unfettered exchanges except among those very close and very trusting. Documentary drama, employing real questions, real responses, live performers, and direct communication with the audience, allows us to greatly widen the range of our unfettered and deeply felt communication.

AFTERWARD

I had the notion to create Answers to Questions I *from research I was doing at the time on the slippery relationship of acting to real-life behavior—which is still one of my pre-occupations and also, quite frankly, was a way of getting to know more about what the post-60s generation of students was thinking about. The result was a 1974 theatre piece that was one of several ushering in a new variety of theatre, which I dubbed at the time "documentary drama," and which has certainly flourished in the ensuing decades, with its most remarkable progenitor at the moment certainly Anna Deveare Smith. For this early venture, Marilyn Mooney (now opera librettist Marilyn Hall) was a crucial collaborator, both in collecting and editing the material, and her involvement permitted me to keep crucially sufficient distance from the data-collection so as not to subvert the evidence with overt professorial presence. The work was performed in 1974 and filmed later that year by Ian Bernard; this article appeared in* The Drama Review *the following year.*

—R.C. 2002

CHAPTER

6

From Middle to Modern Ages

I n the mid-1980s, Edgar Schell and I created a research program with sufficient funding to produce, over a three-year period, 17 cycle plays, mainly from York and Chester, under the composite title The Plaie Called Corpus Christi. *The performances took place in three two-hour segments; I translated the first year's offering (called "The Beginnings") and Schell, with other colleagues, translated the second ("The Nativity") and third ("The Passion"). I served as director/producer of all the plays, while Schell served as dramaturg and played God, literally and figuratively, one might say. In 1990, with funding from the National Endowment for the Humanities, we made a professional video of the N-Towne Passion Play, adapted from our final segment, which continues to be nationally distributed. This essay is only slightly adapted from the one originally published by the Focused Research Program in Medieval Drama in 1986.*

❖ ❖ ❖

The job of a director, in the main, is to preside over certain translations. Translations, for example, from the written to the spoken word, from the general to the specific stage direction, and from "early morning" to "light cue 26." These translations, taken in sum, transform a literary document (words on paper) into a theatrical presentation (actors on stage). The translations accomplished, the director—not himself a participant in the production—goes home, his catalytic operation completed.

Perhaps the biggest translation, certainly in staging a medieval play, is from past to present. For playscripts always come from the past—measured in weeks or years—whereas actors and audiences inhabit a continually self-renewing present. The director must have one foot in both times: he must preserve what is essential in the past, while engaging the attention of the present; he must exhume the past and inspire it with

Originally published in *The Plaie Called Corpus Christi: Focused Research Project in Medieval Drama,* Fall 1985 true breathing. For a stage production lives in its two periods simultaneously: at once in the creative energies of its original authors, and in the fresh interactions of its modern actors and spectators.

Yet the half-millenium that separates our times from the Middle Ages has brought with it enormous changes that a production must somehow bridge: five centuries of evolution (some say deterioration) in the English language, the diversification of European culture, the disappearance of historical and geographic referents, and the breakdown of what was once a unified Western religion by various reformations, lapses, heresies, and schisms.

It would be comforting to think that we could bridge this gap simply by reconstructing these medieval plays in the fashion in which they were originally presented and having our audience view them as preserved objects. This, however, is quite literally impossible—even if we had a firm notion of what the plays initially looked and sounded like, which we don't. The audience, like it or not, is part of the theatrical experience, and I'm afraid that over the centuries we have simply changed too much—in how we speak, what we know, what we believe, and who we are—to apprehend the plays as they were initially meant to be apprehended.

For example, the changes in English pronunciation alone make Middle English—the language of the cycle plays—quite incomprehensible to modern ears; yet if the spoken text is incomprehensible, it cannot fulfill its medieval function, which was to instruct, in an entertaining manner, a popular audience. Yet just by modernizing the original pronunciation we create a wholly new problem; we fatally compromise the verse structure (meter and rhyme) that was also important to the medieval authors. How do we want the modern audience to hear, for example, the four lines following the landfall of the Ark in the play of *Noah:*

Noah's wife: Here haue we beyn, Noy, long enogh
With tray and with teyn, and dreed mekill wogh.
Noah: Behald on this greyn! Nowder cart ne plogh
Is left, as I weyn, nowder tre then bogh.

Modern readers can perhaps make some sense of this, particularly after a little Middle English practice, but no live audience today could begin to understand it in its original pronunciation. Yet if we modernize the pronunciation, the audience can no longer enjoy the rhyming of "enogh" (enough), "wogh" (woe), "plough" (plow), and "bogh" (bough). The once rhyming words have, in the years since they were written, gone their separate ways; the rhymes, on stage at least, are simply irrecoverable. But it is through rhyme that the medieval author asserted the divinity of his story and magic of his dramaturgy. We are stuck: if we translate for the meaning, the rhyme is lost, but if we translate for the rhyme, the meaning is lost; we are thus thrown into a Heisenbergian paradox, knowing only that a popular audience can no longer apprehend meaning and rhyme simultaneously, and that the composite impact of the original language has been irrevocably victimized by linguistic uncertainty!

The same sort of paradox prevails in the staging. We know that the cycles were performed outdoors, in conjunction with a massive outdoor parade, with serial performances taking place on rolling pageant wagons at various "stations" in the city. At York, this parade began at about 4:30 in the morning, lasted well into the night and involved as many as 48 plays performed at up to 16 playing stations. You can walk the parade route in York today and still see the playing places—Mickelgate, Skeldergate, Jubbergate, Girdlergate, Petergate, Coney Street, "John de Gyseburne's door," and "the Pavement"—they are virtually unchanged from the Middle Ages. Upwards of 15,000 spectators would have attended these plays, which were the center of cultural life for many miles around. If we could only reconstruct this event, what an extraordinary medieval festival we would have!

The problem, of course, is not with staging the play, it's with bringing in 15,000 spectators at 4:30 in the morning! It's not that the theatre has changed, *we* have changed.

The processional staging of cycle plays is not, and was never, a "directorial concept;" rather it was an outgrowth of a religious society to which the notion of a secular "theatre" was still unknown; where "plays" were a direct outgrowth of church services and bible readings; where "producers" were civic officers and trade guild (union) leaders; and where the audience simply consisted of everyone in town—and most of those in the neighboring countryside. The 15,000 farmers and tradesmen who came to the York Corpus Christi plays were as crucial to the medieval theatrical experience as were the hundreds of guildmembers and itinerant actors who performed in the plays; the York Corpus Christi play was to York what the Rose Bowl Parade is to Pasadena, Carnival to Rio, and Easter Sunday to Vatican City: a time for mass gatherings and collective cultural celebration.

What we lack today is the mass and the collectivity. We attend the theatre today as individuals, usually in discrete groups (up to a thousand or so) and in discrete time blocks (up to three hours or less). And while the York plays are now performed regularly at York, they are not staged in Micklegate, Jubbergate, or anywhere along the original parade route; they are instead staged—in a three-hour cutting that begins conveniently after dinner—in a much smaller, enclosed space amidst the Abbey ruins outside town. Similarly, the N-Town plays now staged in Lincoln are performed—heavily cut—in the intimacy of the Minster cloister rather than the large square in front of the Cathedral, and the seven hours of York and Wakefield plays currently staged by the National Theatre in London have been divided into three segments, each comfortably performed on a separate evening. Neither the sites nor the times used by medieval producers can be used today, because the medieval audience that occasioned the use of those sites and times no longer exists.

We should also acknowledge that Biblical plays were not originally written to be performed outdoors; they were written to be performed indoors, inside the church, where they were indeed performed for more than 300 years—from the tenth through the thirteenth centuries. The plays only moved outdoors when they became too big, too noisy, and too irreverent to be sustained in sanctified space.

Thus the problem of "historical restoration" takes on deeper complexities. What do we reconstruct—the twelfth-century indoor production, or the fifteenth-century pageant production? And where and when can we reconstruct so as to achieve the same rapport of actor to audience that was envisaged by the original authors? The original authors spoke the same language, worshipped at the same Church, and shared the same moral values as virtually all of their region's inhabitants; when I created an ensemble to produce an extended version of the same play in Southern California, we knew we would enjoy no such affinities with fellow citizens, nor could we expect our production to bring about a moratorium for the California Angels and the Los Angeles Rams, a silencing of the television airwaves, a closing of all other theatres and cinemas, and a universal work stoppage, so that everybody can attend our performances, as everyone in York would have done in 1485! In the ever-busy modern world, we are not the only game in town: that sort of focus is reserved today for global wars and presidential assassinations, not for dramatic inquiries.

So the original staging of medieval cycle plays remains as unrecoverable for us as does the apprehension of the full value of medieval dramatic language; we cannot recreate it simply because we cannot recreate medieval man and his needs, nor medieval society and its values. Thus the need for translation becomes evident. The past must be made to live in the present, and must illuminate and magnify the present. And the present must reveal and animate the past. These are the tasks we have before us.

I have posed, in these remarks, the two major problem areas—language and staging—in which a director is asked to translate a theatrical work from one era to another. The solutions to those problems will surely come in by standing astride the eras and finding their common themes, by reaffirming the medieval spirit with a contemporary morality, by breathing new life into the old—but clearly timeless—human conditions as expressed in these plays.

Whatever the medieval achievement was, it can never be considered primitive or simple-minded. The centuries of peace, the sophisticated social organization, the magnificent cathedral constructions at York, Lincoln, Salisbury, and elsewhere—as well as the vast aesthetic and intellectual concepts that generated the cycle plays—attest to the brilliant and brilliantly disciplined civilization of the High Middle Ages. It is a pleasure to have one foot planted there; it is a demanding task, however, to bridge the eras and try and make these plays come alive in our own times.

CHAPTER

7

Putting a Tree in a Box

I n the winter of 1982-83, Professor Andy Harris of Columbia University called David McDonald in our department with an astounding offer: Jerzy Grotowski was in the U.S. and hoping to come to California, to which end Andy was inquiring if we were interesting in having him speak at Irvine and perhaps a few other UC campuses as well. David brought the proposal to me (I was department chair at the time), and I was beside myself with excitement: in 1965, my first year at UCI, the dean had left on my desk a news story announcing Jerzy's "retirement" from theatre, with note paper-clipped to it (there were no post-its in those days) saying: "Well, Bob, here's what's happened to your hero." So I walked into my acting class that day, about 20 years later, and said to Jim Slowiak, then a UCI directing student and Grotowski devotee (who was soon to become his international acolyte), "Well, Jim, we're bringing you your hero." What goes around comes around.

I had no trouble eliciting a speaking fee from the administration, and invited Jerzy to give a talk, which became two lectures (one on his *Faustus* production, one on his *Theatre of Sources*) and then cooked up some reason to fly to New York to meet him, where Andy Harris set up a luncheon meeting for us at the Players' Club. Jerzy arrived in an ill-fitted suit and tie, greeted me with three kisses on the cheek, and ordered a filet mignon and a small Armagnac. The filet, he explained, was his doctor-ordered diet for a rare blood and/or kidney disease. The three kisses—to be repeated on countless occasions in the coming years—were a Polish tradition. We spoke—wholly in French that day, as his English was still quite wobbly—about a number of peripheral topics: Marcel Marceau, then in town; the current Polish political situation under Jaruzelski; the upcoming speaking tour I had arranged for him; and, finally, his hopes and plans for the immediate future. Suddenly, I realized Jerzy was not merely seeking a speaking tour. He was looking for a new home. Though almost no one knew

Originally published in *Slavic and East European Performance*, Spring 2000 this, he had emigrated to the U.S. He was not to return to Poland for many years.

And he was looking to create a new project. It would be called the Objective Drama project, synthesizing the transcultural research he had begun with his Theatre of Sources and his earlier work as a theatre producer and director. "Traditional Specialists" from around the world would teach ancient ritual performance elements to students—who could then perhaps recombine them into new performances of a prehistoric authenticity. A miracle was about to drop in our laps.

I flew home and started the process of creating a new position for him at UCI. It was a prodigious administrative project. Our department was not then, and is not now, known for radical pedagogical innovation. Our acting teachers had come from conventional theatres or schools: Brewster Mason from the Royal Shakespeare Company, Bill Needles from the Canadian Shakespeare Festival, Curt Conway from the Group Theatre, and three of us (Keith Fowler, Dudley Knight, and myself) from the Yale Drama School. Here was the greatest complementary colleague we could ever find. I assembled the faculty and, with their enthusiastic backing, set about probing the campus administration even before Jerzy arrived. When he did arrive, in March/April 1983, we were already in the thick of negotiations.

We were off to a good start, as Jerzy (surprisingly, I might add) found California quite agreeable. "Mr. Grotowski finds Irvine an inspiring location," I was soon to write, "with inspiring and lively colleagues: he finds in his future collaborators here a 'true Polish family,' and would be very excited about living in this environment for an extended period" (my proposal for "the Objective Drama Institute," April 22, 1983). Nothing in the years to come suggested I had been wrong in this initial assessment.

But everything else was quite a bit more difficult. Creating a place for Grotowski at Irvine, in the Zen phrase conveyed to us by then-dean Robert Garfias, was like "putting a tree in a box." The University, with the countless rigid forms and regulations of a large state institution, was of course the box; Jerzy, the impish Polish guru and luminary, was obviously outside of it—far outside.

The first task, securing a permanent faculty position, turned out to be the easiest part; despite a budget crunch at the time, the University soon granted us a contract at the level of Professor Step VI; this was the highest level appointment our department had ever made—by a full 11 steps on the academic ladder. And it pleased me that salary was the one item in the package that Grotowski accepted immediately and without question.

Everything else, however, he negotiated down to the last semicolon. Jerzy wanted $200,000 per year for expenses, including $25,000 for "props and musical instruments," and $10,000 for telephone charges, substantially more than the entire department was spending on any of these items, then or now). We could offer him barely five percent of those figures. I reminded him that he was famous for creating "poor theatre" in Poland. "The poor theatre," Jerzy replied, "always cost a *lot* of money." It's a phrase I soon came to believe he'd used many times before.

Jerzy was, moreover, unwilling to engage in fundraising, or to write grant proposals, or even to write a definition of this "Objective Drama" that he planned to create. The task of all these duties fell then to me—writing more or less on an "as told to" basis, where Jerzy would talk, in his inimitable blend of French and newly-acquired English, and I would transcribe, re-scribe, and, in general, reshape into what I thought might prove acceptable to university and foundation officials. Then Jerzy would take my draft, share it with counselors still unknown to me, and return it with line-by-line corrections, emendations, and restorations. This went on through innumerable drafts until our proposals acquired an almost mythic inscrutability with unique systems of punctuation and orthography.

We did manage to put our package together, however. A campus-wide "Focused Research Program" provided funds for interdisciplinary research: we therefore submitted a "drama-dance-music-art-anthropology-linguistics program" that eventually brought us $105,000 over three years—enough to create a core program, hire administrative staff, bring in technical ritual specialists (who arrived from Haiti, Japan, Bali, Colombia, and Europe), and provide seed money for additional proposals. And the seedlings indeed emerged: five-figure grants were soon forthcoming from the Rockefeller Foundation, the National Endowment for the Arts, the Shubert Foundation, and from André and Mercedes Gregory.

For his work space, Jerzy wanted just one thing: a barn. During an overnight negotiating session at my house (starting with filet mignon and Armagnac, once again), I told him there were some barns 60 miles east of campus, near the town of Temecula, but that it might be difficult for students to get to them. "Let's go see them now," he said. I noted that it was already two in the morning, but Jerzy insisted. I drew the line: I simply wasn't going on a nighttime sightseeing jaunt—moreover, Jerzy would have to take my refusal as his final answer. Jerzy then became very fond and confidential; his brow wrinkled and his voice dropped into its nether octaves. He asked that the relationship between us be a marriage, not just a partnership. No, I insisted, I was quite well married already, and not prepared to become a bigamist: indeed "Just a partnership" was OK by me. Jerzy harumphed—then twinkled, and we moved to other matters. Finally, with dawn about to break and the Armagnac gone, I caved in. "OK, let's go to Temecula and find a barn," I said, hoping my wife wasn't listening in from the bedroom behind the wall (which of course she was). "No, we don't have to go now" Jerzy said, with a ferocious grin. And he signed the contract I offered him. Just who seduced whom that night, I still can't say.

Amazingly, there was a barn already on the campus, as it turned out, on vacant fields far from the academic plant. Indeed, several other departments had already requested it for various purposes, but we soon managed to secure it exclusively for Grotowski's research, though not without some very angry feelings across campus. We also were granted $69,000 for renovations, and, following Jerzy's specifications, we took out the shabby second floor, installed beautiful hardwood flooring and beams, and painted the interior with the precise shade of light blue that he selected from several dozen samples. We also secured funding to build a wooden "Yurt" adjacent to the Barn: this was to be a space for rest and meditation between work sessions in the Barn. Thus Jerzy had, by this point, two entire buildings solely dedicated to his work. The Focused Research Program in Objective Drama (FRPOD), as it became called, now had its faculty position, funding, and space; soon it also had a technical assistant, Robert Currier (who had initially proposed the Yurt, which was constructed by a company he had dealt with in Northern California), and soon thereafter a full-time administrator, Marian Barnett.

Creating a suitable work schedule now became our biggest headache, as Jerzy insisted the Objective Drama work could only take place during all-night sessions, which were to be arranged on short notice—while of course our students had regularly scheduled classes, rehearsals, jobs, and other assignments that ran almost continuously from 8:00 am to 11:00 pm. This is truly where the box met the tree. There was only one way to resolve this dilemma, and so for two of our three quarters each year we ran parallel drama programs, with 20 selected students studying Objective Drama with Jerzy and his technical specialists in the Barn at night, and the other 200 students studying everything else in regular classrooms during the day. For the Spring quarter, we compromised: Jerzy would teach an occasional afternoon class, or give a lecture, and on weekends would lead his intensive overnight sessions. Happily, however, there was both the good will and sufficient interface to make this all work very well. Despite occasional problems, I learned never to make this sort of detail a sticking point. Otherwise you never will get the tree in the box, and it will be a pretty empty box.

And then we had it. For three years, extraordinary things happened "in the Barn." How do we know? Mostly by hearing it from our students; often by participating in weekend intensives, or in seminars with our drama-dance-music-art-anthropology-linguistics program that were convened from time to time, mainly to satisfy the Focused Research Program's interdisciplinary requirement. Jerzy and I also hosted two public seminars, with observers—some adulatory, some critical—arriving from throughout California. The actual work, which others have described elsewhere, was intense and enthralling. It was not, however, recorded by us, either by videotape or even still photography: a matter of the boss's orders.

Charming and warmhearted in discourse, Jerzy had no private life that I was aware of, outside of his working relationships which were profound and consuming. He was an intense reader and thinker, a classic European intellectual (Martin Buber was a favorite author at the time), and deeply concerned with the onrush of international politics—he was also a great admirer of President Ronald Reagan for confounding the Russian and Polish communist authorities. He almost never went to plays or art events, except that when my wife, Lorna, had a premiere of a play she had written in nearby Long Beach, he asked to attend and did, calling me thereafter "Shakespeare's husband." The three of us had many wonderful dinners and conversations, always ending up on matters concerning "the work." Of course, he knew that he was dying. Once, at dinner in a Mexican restaurant, I caught him staring at the veins on the backs of his hands. "It's amazing," he said upon seeing my gaze, "that the little corpuscles in here are dead." And then he wiggled his fingers playfully.

Jerzy's investigations, which had begun in the conventional theatre and had then moved to the unconventional, had now literally moved to the radical: to the roots of everything in theatre: acting, staging, dramaturgy, and the effusion of an ancient theatrical intensity. He was not interested in the avant-garde (and bristled furiously when people associated him with it, or with "experimental theatre," or with his most hated term of all: improvisation); what he was probing was simply the prehistory of performance, and the prehistory of art. His efforts at UCI were pursued with a most relentless vigor. They never reached their earliest goal—of recombining ancient performance structures into a new but authentic dramaturgy. I deeply regretted that. But they had a profound impact—aesthetic and/or pedagogical—on virtually everyone who experienced them. The early goal, indeed, may ultimately be achieved by those students who are carrying this work—his legacy—into their own performance careers, in "Grotowski Diaspora" companies such as New World Performance Laboratory and Theatre Labyrinth (both in Ohio), which were founded by Grotowski-at-Irvine students and associates. But all of us—our institution, our students, and ourselves—were privileged to be participating colleagues in this absorbing work, and we have been profoundly educated by it.

CHAPTER

8

Patty Hearst: An Actress Identifying with a Part?

The trial of Patty Hearst was one of the most bizarre, and yet dramatically illuminating, juridical events of the tumultuous 1970s. Hearst, an otherwise undistinguished 19-year-old scion of the famed San Francisco publishing family, had been kidnapped from her UC Berkeley apartment by a rag-tag and self-styled "Symbionese Liberation Army"; despite her father's delivery of a seven-figure ransom "to the poor," she was not released and, quite amazingly, soon surfaced at an armed bank heist, assault rifle in hand, now apparently a fired-up associate of her erstwhile captors. Eventually arrested (in a bloodbath that made much of the world for the first time aware of the term "SWAT team"), Hearst argued that she had been essentially brainwashed—that being locked in a closet and repeatedly raped had made her so deranged that she had, at least temporarily, accepted her abductors as new-found, if short-lived, friends. Prosecutors, however, charged her with being a willing SLA convert, and placed the pretty heiress on trial for assisting in the robbery, a decision many in America found even more astonishing than the events themselves. The story, a compendium of sex, crime, money, beauty, generational conflict, and the tail end of hippy/yippie politics, was the tabloid sensation of the year. But it also proved a rare dialectic on the nature of action (inner and outer), and the relation of "criminal intent" and "actor's intention," which I wrote about for the Los Angeles Times *(February 20, 1976), in a piece that was widely republished around the country in the days that followed.*

✦ ✦ ✦

The trial of Patricia Hearst, with its kinky combination of radicalism, sex, terrorism, media hype, antiestablishmentarianism, and a flamboyant cast of characters, happens additionally to raise one of the most intriguing and perplexing questions ever brought to the bar of justice: whether a purported criminal act is essentially physical or mental.

Originally published in the *Los Angeles Times*, 1976

For while popular wisdom tends mindlessly to affirm the famous Frank Loesser lyric, "You can't go to jail for what you're thinking," it is precisely this—what Miss Hearst may or may not have been thinking—that the jury is being asked to determine, for what she was thinking is inextricably linked to the deeds she is charged with having committed.

The physical events seem to be generally uncontested. Miss Hearst was abducted and held for a time in a closet; she subsequently participated in a bank robbery; she engaged in sexual relations with some of her abductors; she failed to take advantage of seemingly safe opportunities to escape—these factors are not being argued.

What is in question is what she was or was not thinking when these events took place. Was she "in love" with a captor, William Wolfe? Did she "willingly" join the SLA? Did she really think the FBI would shoot her on sight?

These are the questions which the jury is being asked to resolve beyond a reasonable doubt. Whether Miss Hearst goes to jail, therefore, will depend almost entirely on what the jury thinks she was thinking. Given what we know about the human mind, this is a very uncomfortable prospect.

How, for example, are we to deal with the possibility of emotional ambivalence? How can we deal, in a court of justice where the scales have but two pans, with the possibility that Miss Hearst had ambivalent rather than absolute feelings about Wolfe, the SLA, the FBI, and her parents? Ambivalence about such matters would hardly be unprecedented even among unabducted adolescents; in Miss Hearst's case, it may be central to the drama.

One of the ironies of the trial is that Miss Hearst is accused, as it were, of having fallen in love with SLA member Wolfe, a charge which she hotly denies, but which surviving SLA "sister" Emily Harris supports. If Miss Hearst was truly "in love," the prosecution implies, she was a willing participant and therefore a guilty one; if she only pretended to "love" Wolfe out of fear for her safety, the defense counters, she was actually an unwilling participant and therefore innocent.

But who can tell the truth here? How would Emily Harris know what was *truly* in Miss Hearst's mind? Would Miss Hearst herself even know for sure? How quantifiable is the feeling of love, or the feeling of past love? How absolute?

If questioned about our own past intimacies, we assess them in the light of whatever elements of enticement, seduction, duress, anxiety, and reward may have accompanied them. How absolute can we be about whether or not they represented "true love"? Nor is it entirely irrelevant who asks such questions of us.

Given the enormous gravity and complexity of Miss Hearst's situation, both at the time of her abduction and now that she is being tried, the notion that she can give an unequivocal and unambivalent assessment of her true feelings for the dead William Wolfe seems beyond all reason.

The principle of cognitive dissonance could explain much of Miss Hearst's behavior during the past two years, but it seems to have no place on the courtroom agenda. Amply studied and defined over the past decade, cognitive dissonance means, quite simply, that people in ambivalent situations often come to believe in what they find themselves doing.

These studies prove what common wisdom has always known: that actors tend to identify with the parts they play, debaters with the positions they are assigned, and attorneys with the claims they are hired to advocate.

Guilt plays a part in this process; a woman who finds herself performing sexual acts with a relative stranger will have a tendency to "justify" those acts to herself by convincing herself that she is in "love" with the man, even though the act was initiated under duress. Similarly, a man who finds himself shouting political slogans will tend to justify that action by coming to believe in the slogans, or believing that he believes in the slogans, even though his shouting was initiated by a hiring agency.

We all may like to think that cognitive dissonance does not apply to us; science reminds us, quite impersonally, that it does. Although the principle may turn out not to be involved in the Hearst case, the chances are very high that it is, and the format of a trial, in any event, affords little room for its proper analysis.

Cognitive dissonance is only one of a series of processes that invariably work to alter our feelings—and our later feelings about those feelings. The defense claim that Miss Hearst was "brainwashed" is patently foolish insofar as we think of brainwashing as a metaphysical restructuring of the mind. It is beyond dispute, however, that Miss Hearst was subjected to persuasion, inducement, seduction, disorientation, and the threat of physical harm. These techniques have great power, resting as they do on mechanisms far beneath the rational workings of consciousness.

The instinct for survival, after all, has given us during the past 100,000 years or so innumerable autonomic responses of compliance: the student nods silent agreement with the arrogant professor, the POW smiles benignly at the prison guard, the rape victim obliges in her indignity. It is absurd to assume that these outward forms of behavior carry no internal ramifications to help make a person's plight more bearable.

In Miss Hearst's situation, all the rewards would come from compliance, and all the punishments from noncompliance or neutrality. If it is clear that Miss Hearst's initial compliance was externally coerced, it is also clear that the pirate-like lifestyle of the SLA, with its brilliant women and daring young men, could eventually exercise a seductive effect on a rich and sheltered young woman.

It would have been extraordinary if the SLA could not have shifted, over the course of Miss Hearst's incarceration, from coercive to seductive control. Control, nevertheless, it remained; whether or not Miss Hearst considered herself willing or unwilling is really not the issue. Miss Hearst's feelings—and her recollection of those feelings—are important but not conclusive. If she felt at the time that she joined the SLA willingly, that may only mean the SLA did a better job on her than we have given it credit for.

The jurors, then, will be asked to find answers that do not exist to questions that are irrelevant. How possibly can they make a judgment? There is only one course open to them: Since they cannot know Miss Hearst's innermost feelings then or now (any more than she can), they will project their own imagined ones.

This is a tricky business, for the jurors may wind up deciding the case on the basis of what each of them considers to be socially approvable conduct.

If they can imagine themselves, at 19, doing pretty much what Miss Hearst did, they will find her innocent. But if the very idea of committing such acts fills them with embarrassment or even shame, they will find her guilty. So, in a sense, when the jurors retire to deliberate, they will be judging not only the defendant but also themselves and their imagined actions.

And, insofar as we, the American public, have made ourselves a larger jury in this case—and have imagined, too, what we would have done in Miss Hearst's situation—we will be judging ourselves as we follow the case down to its most miniscule detail.

CHAPTER

9

Spoken Dialogue in Written Drama

Play dialogue is usually written so as to resemble a form of human conversation (the word "dialogue," indeed, refers both to the interchange of stage speeches and to certain kinds of actual conversations), yet there seem to be substantial structural and syntactical differences between the linguistic interaction of dramatic dialogue, even in naturalistic plays, and the spontaneous give and take of ordinary talk. Play dialogue, for its part, generally consists of logically, paired utterances—question/answer, statement/confirmation, statement/rebuttal—and appears on the page pretty much in complete, orderly sentences. As, for example:

> ANGEL: Whom seek ye in the sepulchre. O Christian women?
> MARYS: Jesus of Nazareth, the crucified. O heavenly one.
> ANGEL: He is not here; He is risen, as he foretold.
> Go announce that he has risen from the sepulchre!
> (*Quem Quaeritis* trope,10th Century A.D.)[1]

or:

> DODGE: Are you having trouble here, Tilden? Are you in some kind of trouble?
> TILDEN: I'm not in any trouble.
> DODGE: You can tell me if you are. I'm still your father.
> TILDEN: I know you're still my father.
> DODGE: I know you had a little trouble back in New Mexico. That's why you came out here.
> TILDEN: I never had any trouble.
> DODGE: Tilden, your mother told me all about it.
> TILDEN: What'd she tell you?
> (*Buried Child*, Sam Shepard, 1978)[2]

Originally published in *Essays in Theatre*, Spring 1986

But real conversation, if transcribed onto the page, would look nothing at all like this. Real conversation lacks this clear, logical, *literary* form; typically, it looks instead something like this:

P: Moore heard the testimony and said well you're not—

E: He was never asked the right questions. Now, as far as he—

H: He probably didn't to the Grand Jury, either.

E: That's right. As far as the quality of the evidence is concerned—(Material unrelated to Presidential actions deleted) Well, to go back to the—

P: All right. I only mentioned (unintelligible) because, let me—go ahead with your—

E: Well, all I was going to say is that—

P: All right. I now have evidence that—

E: You don't have evidence if I—

("Watergate" tape: transcribed conversation between President Nixon [P], Robert Haldeman [H] and John Erlichman [E], 1972. Although the Watergate tapes hardly represent "typical" uses of spoken language, they are the most substantial extant body of covertly recorded and transcribed human conversations.)[3]

Clearly, spoken conversation is structured by a different son of syntax than the dramatic structure of the *Quam Quaeritis* trope and most subsequent dramas.

Keir Elam, who has investigated this matter, contrasts a snatch of actual conversation overheard in a coffee shop with a fragment from a typical modern American play, and notes that whereas the real-life conversation "progresses through incomplete and dangling sentences, false starts, and repetition," the play fragment, "although scarcely elaborate syntactically, falls into well demarcated units."[4] Elam concludes that "Dramatic dialogue generally proceeds through syntactically complete or self-sufficient utterances, while 'everyday' exchanges are less neatly segmented."[5]

Spoken conversation, however, may have its own syntax. Conversation analysts, over the past two decades, have identified a growing variety of conversational hitches and ploys, and departures from literary syntax, that occur regularly in speech but are rarely found in the reconstructed speech of most novels, nonfiction narratives, news accounts or plays. Erving Goffman, in his recent *Forms of Talk*, lists four categories of "speech faults" routine to talking but rare in writing (even that writing which is supposed to be a transcription of talking); these include *influencies*, which are "hitches in the smooth flow of syntactically connected words, as with restarts, filled pauses, stuttering;" *slips,* which are "words or their parts that have gotten mixed up, or misuttered, as in word transposition, phonological disturbance, and the like;" *boners,* which are malapropisms of various kinds, and *gaffes,* which are "unintended and unknowing breaches in 'manners' or some norm of 'good' conduct—thus: indiscretions, tactlessness, indelicacy, irreverence, immodesty, intrusiveness, etc."[6] Goffman also discusses non-word utterances, such as grunts of approval or disapproval, sexual moans, confirmation hums, "ahs" and other such vocalizations, and develops a model of "talk" that has a fully interactional, superliterary syntax. "Natural conversation," he says, "is not subject to systematic transformation into words. What is basic to natural talk might not be a conversational unit at all, but an interactional one, [some of which] . . . is quite likely not to involve speech at all."[7]

The structural organization of actual conversation is also far less regular than it is in most written reconstructions of such conversations, and the paired utterances customary in written dialogue are far more rare. In real conversation, dialogue is not contrived to reach an author's predetermined dramaturgical ends, and the neat balancings of questions and answers, statements, confirmations and rebuttals are not so neatly packaged. In a play, the characters speak when the playwright wants them to; in actual conversation, by contrast, individuals must *compete* for the right to speak, in a process which conversation analysts call "turn-taking" or "floor apportionment." Winning and holding the floor—that is to say, gaining and sustaining the opportunity to speak—is often more pragmatically significant to conversation analysis than what is actually said. The battle for the floor, which in actual conversation leads to interruptions, overrides, overlaps, speech halts, simultaneous speech starts, fadeaways and under-the-breath mumblings, plays a much more crucial role in conversation than in most literary reconstructions of such conversation.

Both Goffman and Elam suggest that dramaturgical or literary necessity may prevent playwrights from creating dialogue conforming to a truly conversational structure. Goffman, for example, points out that "(purely) *verbal* exchanges may be the natural trait of plays . . . and other forums of literary life wherein words can be transcribed much more effectively than actions can be described.[8] Elam notes that in a play, ". . . turn-taking rights are established on dramaturgical grounds rather than on democratic conversational principles . . . . Thus the kind of battles for the floor which occur in extra-dramatic conversation, whereby potential next-speakers attempt to 'book' the right to talk by overlapping or echoing the current speaker, asking permission to interrupt, overriding other would-be speakers, etc., . . . are circumvented in the drama through the need to focus on the major figures, to allow them as much talking space as they require . . . to follow their contributions one at a time, etc."[9]

Yet conversational structure has always provided at least a partial basis for the language of the stage, and some violations of literary syntax, irregularly segmented utterances and turn-taking gambits have been associated with the earliest dramas. Slips and gaffes are prevalent in Aristophanic and Plautine comedy, and in the earliest medieval plays. Boners are a staple of Elizabethan comedy, and are commonly personified by the 18th-century dramatic character—Mrs. Malaprop—who eponymously exhibited them. Non-word utterances are in Shakespeare, either from the author's hand or via actors' interpolations that found their ways into published versions. The "inarticulate hero" of mid-century American drama was a creature virtually defined by bad grammar and speech faults, and his non-literary mumblings became a caricature of a certain style of American dramatic writing (as well as acting) a generation or two ago.

Indeed, a fairly comprehensive taxonomy of Goffman's speech influencies and Elam's incomplete and dangling sentences can be extracted from the Shakespearean canon. Let us look, for example, at Shakespeare's sentence fragments—specifically those denoted by a dash in their original punctuation. The use of the dash, indicating a broken sentence, is fairly common in the Shakespeare First Folio, appearing in 19 plays.[10]

Where dashes occur (and they are long dashes in the Folio, usually five or six cms in length) they always denote a speaking break, in any of thirteen categorizable conversational hitches:

1. a character interrupting another (the most common), as:

> *Henry:* And if the rest be true, which I have heard
> Thou came'st——
> *Richard:* I'll hear no more:
> Die, prophet in thy speech *(stabs him)*
> $\qquad\qquad\qquad$ (*Henry VI. Part III. V.vi.55-57*)[11]

2. a character dying in mid-speech:

> *Cleopatra*: O Anthony! ay I will take thee too.

What should I stay——*(dies)*
(*Antony & Cleopatra.* V.ii.315-16)

3. a character physically prevented from continuing:

Panthino: Tut, man: I mean thou'lt lose the flood, and in losing the flood, lose thy voyage, and in losing thy voyage, lose thy master, and in losing thy master, lose thy service, and in losing thy service——why dost thou stop my mouth?
(*Two Gentleman of Vero*na. II.iii.46-51)

4. an interruption caused by a new arrival on stage:

Grumio: E'en at hand, alighted by this: and therefore be not——Cock's passion, silence. I hear my master.
(*The Taming of the Shrew.* IV.i.120-21)

5. a restart; that is, a character stopping in midsentence and deciding to say something else:

Iago: Nothing my Lord; or if——I know not what.
(*Othello*, III.iii.36)

6. a trail-off; that is, a character losing interest in completing his or her sentence:

Hamlet: The body is with the King, but the King is not with the body.
The King, is a thing——
Guildenstern: A thing my Lord?
Hamlet: Of nothing.
(*Hamlet*, IV.ii.29-31)

7. a trail-off, followed by a restart:

Hamlet: For if the Sun breed maggots in a dead dog, being a good kissing carrion——Have you a daughter?
(*Hamlet*, II.ii.181-83)

8. moving out of an aside, or a change of intended hearer:

> *Edmund*: [*aside*] Pat: he comes like the catastrophe of the old comedy: my cue is
> villainous melancholy, with a sigh like Tom o'Bedlam.———[*to Edgar*]
> O these eclipses do portend these divisions.
>> *(King Lear,* I.ii.145-49)

9. a nervous flutter:

> *Mistress Quickly:* I shall never laugh but in that maid's company: but (indeed) she
> is given too much to alicholy and musing: but for you———well———go to———
>> *(Merry Wives.* I.iv.162-65)

10. one character finishing another's sentence:

> *Parolles:* Right, as 'twere a man assured of a———
> *Lafeu:* Uncertain life, and sure death.
>> *(All's Well That Ends Well*, II.iii.19-20)

11. a reflective pause:

> *Posthumous:* [*being shown the bracelet*] Jove———
> Once more let me behold it: Is it that
> Which I left with her?
>> *(Cymbeline,* II.iv.99-100)

12. a character afraid to continue:

> *Messenger:* [*bringing Antony bad news*] And to Ionia, whilst———
> *Antony:* Antony thou wouldst say.
> *Messenger:* Oh my Lord.
> *Antony:* Speak to me home. Mince not the general tongue.
>> *(Antony and Cleopatra,* I.ii.107-09)

13. a character choked and stammering from guilt:

> *Clarence:* Who sent you hither? Wherefore do you come?
> *2nd Murderer:* To, to, to——
> *Clarence:* To murder me?
> *Both murderers:* Aye, aye.
>
> (*Richard III.* I.iv. 176-79)

Clearly Shakespeare tailored his plays with a wide variety of speech faults—particularly influencies, but also false starts, boners, slips and gaffes—and developed, in his dialogue, elements of non-literary conversational structure; indeed, it could be said that among Shakespeare's many accomplishments, from a craft standpoint, was the successful conversationalization of blank verse, which in earlier writers, from Sackville and Norton to Christopher Marlowe, was as regular syntactically as it was metrically.

The broken sentence or speech halt, typographically reproduced in the Folio text by a dash, is nowhere in the drama more effective than it is in *King Lear,* where the breakdown of Lear's sentences mirrors the collapse of his power:

> *Lear:* Fiery? The fiery Duke, tell the hot Duke that——
>   No, but not yet, maybe he is not well.
>
> (II.iv.105-06)

and, later in the same scene:

> *Lear:* No, you unnatural hags,
>   I will have such revenges on you
>   That all the world shall——-I will do such things.
>   What they are yet, I know not, but they shall be
>   The terrors of the earth!
>
> (II.v.281-85)[12]

Lear's influencies are devastating; he cannot finish his sentences with authority as he cannot finish his life with dignity. But Lear's speech halts, which are a result of his impotence (political as well as psychological), are poised against the powerfully obnoxious and deliberate trail-off of the steward Oswald:

Lear: You you Sirrah, where's my daughter?
(enter Steward)
Oswald: So please you——*(exit)*
Lear: What says the fellow there?

(I.iv.49)

Oswald's dash, representing the fealty not delivered, the deliberate snub, speaks a volume in its pure silence.

Still elsewhere in the play, speech halts and interrupts become the repeated motifs of an aborted reign, a disjointed family, and the bankruptcy of logical, literary syntax:

Lear: I can scarce speak to thee, thou'lt not believe
    With how depraved a quality——O Regan!

(II.iv.139-40)[13]

Albany: I cannot be so partial, Goneril,
    To the great love I bear you——
Goneril: Pray you, content.

(I.iv.334-36)

Lear: O Regan, Goneril!
    Your old kind father, whose frank heart gave all——
    Oh, that way madness lies, let me shun that.

(III.iv.18-20)

Gentleman: [*showing a knife*] 'Tis hot, it smokes, it came even from the heart of——O she's dead.

(V.iii.223-25)

Shakespeare's use of conversational structures and motifs in *King Lear* is particularly intrinsic to the poetry and the human passions of the play, forging, as they do, a link between the final inexpressiveness of formal language with the profundity of pre-verbal feeling and design. But conversational structures and syntaxes are not peculiar to profundity or archetypal tragedy. Fast-paced and highly comic floor battles were also Shakespeare's medium, if not his invention, as in this scene from *All's Well That Ends Well*, part of which was quoted above:

Lafeu: To be relinquished of the artists——
Parolles: So I say.
Lafeu: Both of Galen and Paracelsus——
Parolles: So I say.
Lafeu: Of all the learned and authentic fellows——
Parolles: Right; so I say.
Lafeu: That gave him out incurable——
Parolles: Why, there 'tis; so say I too.
Lafeu: Not to be helped——
Parolles: Right; as 'twere, a man assured of a——
Lafeu: Uncertain life, and sure death.
Parolles: Just, you say well; so would I have said.
Lafeu: I may truly say, it is a novelty to the world.
Parolles: It is, indeed, if you will have it in showing, you shall read it in——what do ye call there?
Lafeu: A showing of a heavenly effect in an earthly actor.
Parolles: That's it; I would have said the very same.
Lafeu: Why your dolphin is not lustier: for me I speak in respect——
Parolles: Nay 'tis strange, 'tis very strange, that this is the brief and the tedious of it, and he's of a most facinerious spirit, that will not acknowledge it to be the——
Lafeu: Very hand of heaven.
Parolles: Aye, so I say.
Lafeu: In a most weak——
Parolles: And debile minister, great power great transcendence: which should, indeed, give us a further use to be made than alone the recovery, of the king, as to be——
Lafeu: Generally thankful.
Parolles: I would have said it; you say well.

(II.iii.10-45)[14]

Floor battles are the commonest expression of conflict, and dramatic situations represent not just a conflict of ideas, but a conflict of individuals each trying to express those ideas. Characters in plays strive not only to win objectives, they strive to win the floor in order to win their objectives. Such strivings constitute the life of the drama, resulting not only in escalating arguments, but also the mounting crescendos of passion, poetry, rhetoric and hilarity which we associate with exciting theatre. But floor battles follow written grammars. Shakespeare's dashes (or his editors') attempt to guide the actor into the peculiarly theatrical syntax of the spoken word.

The exploration and exploitation of conversational structures has seen a quantum leap in the last twenty years of dramatic writing. A host of contemporary playwrights have absorbed and replicated these conversational grammars, and have radically expanded our notions of the possibilities of dramatic dialogue, creating new spoken syntaxes that follow the patterns that Goffman describes.

Tennessee Williams, in one of his last full length plays *(In the Bar of a Tokyo Hotel,* 1969)* experiments boldly with influencies, particularly incomplete sentences, which constitute about sixty percent of the play's dialogue. For example:

MARK: I'll.
MIRIAM: You'll stay here with your work.
MARK: It could be a fantasy that I'm.
MIRIAM: Shattering a frontier?
MARK: In my room is a suit I've never worn. A shower takes me two minutes. I'll be down in five.
MIRIAM: I won't be seen today with a man that.
MARK: I've always felt that. After the work, so little is left of me. To give to another person.
MIRIAM: Mark.
MARK: Miriam.
MIRIAM: Go back to the States. Enter a. Consult a. As your wife, I.
MARK: I can't interrupt the.[15]

Willlams makes no attempt to punctuate these exchanges in a way that would be helpful to the reader (or the actor) and ends each sentence fragment with a simple period, thus refusing to distinguish between sentences abandoned by the speaker from those cut off by another's interruption. More recent playwrights, when they have broken with conventional literary syntax, have wrestled a bit more with matters of punctuation and page presentation, so as to clarify the nature of the segmentations of the dialogue, and the inter-character floor-apportionment. Trevor Griffiths, in *Thermidor* (1971), includes in parentheses the ends of speeches cut off by an interruption:

YUKHOV: There's very little to be done about anything, once charges have been laid and . . . (due legal processes set in motion).
ANYA: Charges? What charges?
YUKHOV: Comrade Pakhanova . . . (I have been trying to tell you . . .).
ANYA: What charges? I know nothing about charges.
YUKHOV: I'm trying to tell you, Comrade . . .
ANYA: You said nothing about charges. There was nothing... (on the card about charges . . .).
YUKHOV: *(fist)* Will you listen to me![16]

Arthur Kopit, in *Wings* (1979), depicts his heroine's aphasia by parallel columns of text: one being Mrs. Stilson's voice, one being extraneous sounds as heard by her:

SOUNDS OUTSIDE HER-
SELF VOICES: (garbled) Just
relax./No one's going to hurt
you./Can you hear us?/Be careful!/
You're hurting her!

MRS. STILSON'S VOICE
What's my name? I don't know
my name! Where's my arm? I
don't have an arm![17]

For *Top Girls* (1983) Caryl Churchill invented a notation system for the radically segmented dialogue she wrote: a slash (/) indicates when one character starts speaking before the other is finished, or when a character continues speaking right through another's speech, and an asterisk indicates when a speech follows on from a speech earlier than the one immediately before it. Thus:

NIJO: Don't you like getting dressed? I adored my clothes./When I was chosen to give sake to His Majesty's brother.

MARLENE: You had prettier colours than Isabella.

NIJO: The Emperor Kameyana, on his formal visit, I wore raw silk pleated trousers and a seven-layered gown in shades of red, and two outer garments./yellow lined with green and a light

MARLENE: Yes, all that silk must have been very . . .

JEAN: I dressed as a boy when I left home.*

NIJO: Green jacket. Lady Betto had a five-layered gown in shades of green and purple.

ISABELLA: *You dressed as a boy?

MARLENE: Of course. / for safety.

JOAN: It was easy, I was only twelve./ Also women weren't allowed in the library. We wanted to study in Athens.

MARLENE: You ran away alone?

JOAN: No, not alone. I went with my friend./He was sixteen

NIJO: Ah, an elopement.

JOAN: but I thought I knew more science than he did . . .[18]

David Mamet, in *Glengarry Glen Ross* (1983), uses a unique combination of ellipsis, capitals, italics, triple exclamation points, and omitted punctuation to denote the host of slips, gaffes, influencies, restarts, interruptions, broken words, abbreviated words, imbedded questions (questions within questions), body language, repetitions, non-word utterances, and, most particularly, obscenities in his recapitulation of businessmen in the heat of argument:

ROMA: Oh, Fuck. Fuck. FUCK FUCK FUCK! WILLIAMSON!!! WILLIAMSON!!! OPEN THE FUCKING . . . WILLIAMSON...

BAYLEN: Who are you?

WILLIAMSON: They didn't get the contracts.

ROMA: Did they . . .

WILLIAMSON: They got, listen to me . . .

ROMA: Th . . .

WILLIAMSON: Listen to me: They got some of them.

ROMA: Some of them . . .

BAYLEN: Who told you . . . ?

ROMA: Who told me wh . . . ? You've got a fuckin', you've . . . a . . . who is this . . . ? You've got a board-up on the window . . . *Moss* told me.

BAYLEN: Moss . . . Who told him?

ROMA: How the fuck do *I* know? (To Williamson) *What . . . talk* to me.

WILLIAMSON: They took *some* of the con . . .

ROMA: . . . some of the contracts . . . Lingk. James Lingk. I closed . . .

WILLIAMSON: You closed him yesterday.

ROMA: *Yes.*

WILLIAMSON: It went down. I filed it.

ROMA: You did?

WILLIAMSON: Yes.

ROMA: Then I'm over the fucking top and you owe me a Cadillac.

WILLIAMSON: I . . .

ROMA: and I don't want any fucking shit and I don't give a shit. Lingk puts me over the top, you filed it, that's fine, any other shit kicks out *you* go back. You . . . *you* reclose it. 'cause I *closed* it and you . . . me the car.

BAYLEN: Would you excuse us, please.

AARONOW: I, um, and may . . . maybe they're in . . . they're in . . . you should, John, if we're ins . . .[19]

The broken sentences of these plays create undeniable dramatic problems, not the least of which is that they make the play hard to read, and therefore hard to stage—even for actors and directors quite used to reading plays in manuscript. New forms of orthography seem to be required in making these plays comprehensible as working scripts. The irregulary segmented dialogue creates certain dramaturgical problems as well. Gregory and Carroll have suggested that "When the actor performs, having learnt his lines and rehearsed them, he is speaking what is written to be spoken as if not written . . . This mode of speech . . . has many markers similar to speech but it is not, of course, identical with it . . . if the actor on the stage spoke as people do in 'real life,' with frequent *non sequiturs*, false starts, allusions, digressions, sentence fragments, etc., two things would be likely to happen: the audience would suspect that the actor had failed to learn his lines; and, more importantly, perhaps, the audience would be unlikely to be getting the information it needs to get, in order that the 'two hours' traffic of the stage' emerges as a whole and understandable experience.[20] Some of these "conversational" plays do indeed face these problems.[21]

What theatrical or literary effect may be lost through the adoption of a truly conversational structure, however, is often more than compensated for by the added vigor, lifelikeness, and psychological intricacies of the more freewheeling syntax of spoken language, and the irregularly segmented speeches of actual conversation. Indeed, we must realize that dramatic dialogue is not first and foremost a literary medium, it is rather a language of sounds, moves, gestures, poses, and various human interactions, in which semantic meaning and literary formalities are certainly ingredients, but not, necessarily the dominating ones. Drama, which is generally an art in which people talking (actors) simulate people talking (characters), does not have to depend on literary grammars; drama creates its own syntax. The dramatic power of plays which capture the full psychophysiological spectrum of human interaction can be both profound and immense; it is hard otherwise to account for the critical success of works such as *Glengarry Glen Ross.*

The lifelikeness of conversational syntax lends drama an authenticity, but this should not be confused with mere naturalism. Certainly the adoption of conversational structure lends a strength to naturalistic dialogues: *Glengarry Glen Ross,* which has been skillfully wrought in its depiction of a (possibly fanciful) Chicago patois, seems, when enacted with similar skill, extraordinarily true to the life of a certain class of characters. But verisimilitude is not the principal achievement of conversational dialogue structure, which, indeed, can be used effectively in quite non-naturalistic plays. Caryl Churchill's above-cited dialogue from *Top Girls,* for example, transpires between a thirteenth-century Buddhist nun, a ninth-century Pope, and a contemporary British executive; the dialogue has a human persuasiveness and a social dynamic that makes Churchill's fantasy both exciting and engaging. The adoption of conversational structure is a humanizing, not a naturalizing feature of the drama. It brings onto the stage the timeless psychological matrices of human communication, and the social dynamics of verbal interaction, and allows the playwright to develop characters not simply by talking through and about them, but by creating a whole system of talk—in all its real-world complexity, and with its full complement of influencies and imprecisions. It is, then, perhaps best to look at dramatic dialogue as an interactional form poised between a literary/verbal construct on the one hand, and an imitation (in the Aristotelian sense) of multi-dynamic, interpersonal conversation on the other.

Historically, one supposes, neither side of the equation has priority. Written rituals, narrative poems, literary sources, and religious rites lie at the source of the most ancient plays; but the "playing" of children, where they imitate the conversations and interactions of their elders, is equally antediluvian, What ties the two together—and has from time immemorial—is the actor. It is the actor's function to turn the literature of the drama into the life of the theatre; to make the abstract real and the literary human and dynamic. There is an interesting etymological point here. The original Greek word for the actor is *hypokrite,* which originally meant "answerer." That is, the Greek actor "answered" the choral ode, and was, therefore, paired with the chorus. But as Aeschylus added a second actor, and Sophocles a third, mere "answering" was not enough. Two-person and three-person dialogue became the principal verbal medium of the theatre, and the job of the *hypokrite* became not simply to provide his half of a set of paired utterances, but to recreate the complexities of free-wheeling, give-and-take, *competitive* conversations—filled, as in actual conversations, with a whole taxonomy of slips and gaffes. Thus the actor's art has been enlarged to include the embodiment of a whole speaking person, not just an answerable set of orated notions. And this has led us to the modern meaning of the *hypokrite*: a dissembler. The actor not only plays (dissembles) a character he is not, he impersonates that character as a whole human being, and he enacts, as his own, the whole of a character's interactions. He has transcended mere answering as the drama has transcended the question/answer, statement/rebuttal format; he is now engaged in a complex and multidimensional human interaction, most of which is seen through a spoken dialogue whose syntax derives in part from literary contrivance and in part from the illiteracies of social speech.

The tension between literary and conversational grammars has, in the best examples, created a dramatic dialogue that is both shapely and interactive; both focused and allusive; both logically precise and humanly spasmodic. The more radical absorption of conversational structure into dramatic dialogue in recent years has permitted a drama that is capable of moving into the silences of daily life, and of reaching some conflicts which cannot be verbalized, conflicts for which there is no answer nor no answering, but only a lucid confusion; a grappling for the floor, a stammering of ideas, a taxonomy of influencies, a lexicon of slips and gaffes, and, from time to time, a desperate struggle to complete sentences.

NOTES

1 In, among many others, Robert Cohen, *Theatre* (Palo Alto: 1981), .p. 96.

2 Sam Shepard, *Buried Child,* in *Seven Plays* (New York: 1981), p. 70.

3 The Presidential Transcripts (New York: 1974), p. 249. Apart from its political signifi-cance, this volume is an extraordinary treasure of data for conversation analysis, inas-much as ethical, legal, financial, and practical restraints make the surreptitious recording and subsequent transcribing of actual conversation on this scale all but impossible. In the case of these transcripts, the secret recording device—which was automatically engaged whenever anyone spoke—had been in place for so long that even those who were knowledgeable of its existence (Nixon and Haldeman) would be speaking pretty much as if oblivious to its existence.

4 Keir Elam, *The Semiotics of Theatre and Drama* (New York: 1980), p. 180.

5 *Ibid.*

6. Erving Goffman, *Forms of Talk* (Philadelphia: 1981), pp. 200-10.

7 *Ibid.*, p.48.

8 *Ibid.*

9 Elam, pp. 181-82.

10 Usually once, rarely more than three times. There are no dashes in the Folio printings of *I Henry VI, Titus Andronicus, Romeo and Juliet, Measure for Measure, Comedy of Errors, Much Ado About Nothing. Love's Labor's Lost, A Mid-summer Night's Dream, The Merchant of Venice, As You Like It, Twelfth Night, The Winter's Tale, King John, 2 Henry IV,* or *Henry V.* No particular claim is made here that Folio punctuation should have priori-ty consideration over Quarto punctuation, or even the

punctuation of modern editions; however Folio punctuation, since much of it comes from the playhouse versions, is generally a good starting point for acting/staging pur-poses.

11 Punctuation in this, and the succeeding Shakespearean fragments, is as printed in the First Folio except where noted. Spelling, however, and speech heads are modernized.

12 In rhetoric, an aposiopesis, "a sudden breaking off of a sentence for emotional empha-sis." Lear's speech halts, as punctuated in Quarto and Folio versions, are discussed by Steven Urkowitz in *Shakespeare's Revision of King Lear* (Princeton, 1980), from whence the above definition (p. 18).

13 This, and the next three fragments, are as punctuated in the G.B. Harrison edition (New York: 1952).

14 As punctuated in Harrison, above.

15 Tennessee Williams, *In the Bar of a Tokyo Hotel* (New York: 1969), pp. 22-23.

16 Trevor Griffiths, *Apricots & Thermidor* (London: 1978), p. 19.

17. Arthur Kopit, *Wings* (New York: 1978), p. 31.

18 Caryl Churchill, *Top Girls* (New York: 1984), p. 8.

19 David Mamet, *Glengarry Glen Ross* (New York: 1984), pp. 53-55.

20 Michael Gregory and Susanne Carroll. *Language and Situation: Language Varieties and their Social Contexts* (London: 1978), pp. 42-43.

21 A reviewer of the author's 1983 production of *In the Bar of a Tokyo Hotel,* while praising the acting highly, wondered in print if the actors hadn't forgotten their lines from time to time. They hadn't, but Gregory and Carroll's prediction proved true.

SECTION 2 TWO

On Plays

CHAPTER

10

Shakespeare's Sixteen-Year-Old Hamlet

*T*he following two essays on Hamlet, first written in the 1970s, argue that Shakespeare
intended Hamlet to be sixteen years old, and that there may be specific textual
*evidence, among other indications, to support this. I cannot pretend that this viewpoint has
taken hold in the scholarly community, or even among my friends; I am not aware of a single
published citation—or even an informal comment or email to their author—that so much as
refers to either of these essays since they were originally published. But once more into the
breach: Nothing, including seeing whole handfuls of Hamlets since concocting this notion, has
made me change my conviction about any of it.*

Along with many other critics, I have always considered Prince Hamlet to have
been a boy. A real boy, too; not a man at all, but an adolescent on the verge of achieving manhood; perhaps as young as sixteen or so. This feeling, if it could be proven,
would explain what seem to be several difficulties in the play: it would explain why
Hamlet did not simply ascend the Danish throne upon his father's death; it would
explain why Hamlet is still a "school-fellow" of Horatio's at Wittenberg, and it would
explain why both Laertes and Polonius can dismiss Hamlet's suit to Ophelia as mere
puppy love:

LAERTES: For Hamlet, and the trifling of his favour,
Hold it a fashion and a toy in blood,
A violet in the youth of primy nature.[1]

POLONIUS: For Lord Hamlet,

Originally published in *Educational Theatre Journal*, May 1973

Believe so much in him that he is young.

Other obvious elements in the text support this as yet unproven interpretation. Polonius continues to call Hamlet a "youth," and of the "younger sort"; he construes Hamlet's antics as "pranks," and suggests sending Hamlet to his mother for what we would today consider a scolding. The king considers Hamlet's grief "unmanly," and Laertes thinks Hamlet's importunings to his sister "unmast'red." Ophelia calls Hamlet "that unmatched form and feature of blown youth," and in the First Quarto, Gertrude calls at her son, "How now boy!"[2] The very first time we hear of Hamlet in the play, he is called "young Hamlet," and while the adjective serves to distinguish him from his late father of the same name, it also connotes a definite feeling of youthfulness which lingers throughout the rest of the play.

Critics have long questioned Hamlet's age. About 100 years ago two German critics wrote of Hamlet's "unripe youth," which they found suggested by his "inner qualities, this all embracing pain (*weltschmerz),* this pessimism, which springs from idealism, this blazing up of quickly excited passion, this irresolute endurance of evil treatment, this yearning for the superlative and overlooking the positive, this continual carping and wanting everything better, this self-esteem with constant self-disparagement, and all the thousand things which betray youth and excuse it, all show Hamlet as a very young prince."[3] Two years later another critic suggested that Hamlet's action "is not the weak and petulant action of an emasculated man of thirty, but the daring, wilful, defiant action of a high-spirited, sensitive youth, rudely summoned from the gay pursuits of youth."[4] This feeling has persisted in *Hamlet* criticism up to the present day; it is noteworthy that among the less controversial suggestions in Eleanor Prosser's 1971 study is the assertion that "He is very young in these early scenes, perhaps only eighteen."[5]

Yet the textual evidence of V.i has heretofore stood in stark opposition to these more subjective judgments. Here, in the graveyard, apparently in no mistaken terms, the clown (gravedigger) calmly tells us that Hamlet is no less than thirty years old. He does this first by declaring that he has been digging graves since the day of Hamlet's birth, and second by saying, "I have been sexton here man and boy thirty years." So by the rudimentary A=B, B=C, A=C, we find that Hamlet is thirty. And as if to confirm this piece of information, the clown takes a skull from the earth that "hath lien you i'th'earth three-and-twenty years," and Hamlet looks upon the object and exclaims, "Alas, poor Yorick. I knew him Horatio." If Hamlet knew a man dead twenty-three years, and if, in fact, he remembered being kissed in the lips and carried by that man, as he goes on to say, then Hamlet must be at least twenty-seven or so.

Thus there seems to be a direct conflict in Hamlet between the intuitive feelings of many readers and scholars and the information of the fifth act. Many critics have tried to tackle this difficulty head on. V. Osterberg, in a book entitled *Prince Hamlet's Age*, argues that the Graveyard Scene was intended purely for entertainment, not for factual analysis, and that "thirty" and "three-and-twenty" were just nice, arbitrary, and convenient mouthfuls of words which worked with the rhythm of their respective lines.[6] Adolphus Jack has speculated, in a more recent book, that Shakespeare intended Hamlet to be somewhat younger, but "aged" him because of the profundity of the soliloquies.[7] It has even been argued that "The poet in the Fifth Act had forgot what he wrote in the First,"[8] and that ten years are supposed to "elapse between the beginning of the play and its conclusion."[9] Other critics have simply suggested that Hamlet's literal age makes no difference to the play whatever. None of these solutions, however, seems to give much satisfaction to the reader or scholar, much less to the actor or director.

A more acceptable interpretation of Hamlet's apparent age discrepancy is that Shakespeare found it convenient to describe Hamlet as young in the First Act and older in the Fifth, thus illustrating metaphorically his maturation during the course of the play. Shakespeare, writing for the stage and not the library, had the freedom of juggling reality in favor of a sound dramatic effect; the original Globe audience, unlike the present-day reader, could not flip back the pages. Elmer Edgar Stoll proposes this point of view, suggesting that there are many "loose ends and ragged edges"[10] in the plays of Shakespeare, including Cassio's presumed wife and Lady Macbeth's presumed children, and that Hamlet's youth is a presumption that Shakespeare begins with and conveniently ignores as the play draws to its close. Stoll concludes that Shakespeare, who was not a classicist, paid his allegiance "to the demands of imagination . . . not to the demands and scruples of art."[11] I find Stoll's interpretation the best of those available, but still puzzling. Why would Shakespeare come up with anything even *like* thirty as an age for Hamlet, even in the Fifth Act? At thirty, particularly in the Renaissance, Hamlet would be eligible to be a *grandfather*, and this accelerated maturation seems unfitting for Hamlet, even as a metaphor. I have sought to find evidence that Shakespeare never intended the whole thirty-years-old business, and while my mission was not dispassionate in its pursuit, I think my findings may bear objective consideration.

Here is the original First Folio text for the pertinent scene between Hamlet and the Clown in V.i:

HAMLET: How long hast thou been a Grave-maker?

CLOWN: Of all the dayes i'th'yeare, I came too't that day that our last King *Hamlet* o'recame *Fortinbras.*

HAMLET: How long is that since?

CLOWN: Cannot you tell that? every foole can tell that: It was the very day, that young *Hamlet* was borne, hee that was mad, and sent into England.

HAMLET: I marry, why was he sent into England?

CLOWN: Why, because he was mad; hee shall recover his wits there; or if he do not, it's no great matter there.

HAMLET: Why?

CLOWN: 'Twill not be seene in him, there the men are as mad as he.

HAMLET: How came he mad?

CLOWN: Very strangely they say.

HAMLET: How strangely?

CLOWN: Faith e'ene with loosing his wits.

HAMLET: Upon what ground?

CLOWN: Why heere in Denmarke: I have bin sixeteene heere, man and Boy thirty yeares.[12]

Of course the astonishing word in this passage is "sixeteene." The First Folio definitely suggests with this line that the clown has been "heere" (that is, upon this ground-in Denmark-as a grave-maker) for sixteen years. The clown has added the somewhat extraneous information that he has been *alive* (man and Boy) for thirty years, which means that he began his trade when he was fourteen, a reasonable assumption. The A=C of this line is, of course, that Hamlet is sixteen years old! But this quite sensible First Folio reading has been entirely ignored for the past three hundred and fifty years.

The standard reading of the line in question originated in the Second Quarto of *Hamlet,* published in 1604/05, and routinely accepted as the most accurate early edition of the play, transcribed and composed from Shakespeare's autograph copy.[13] The Second Quarto rendition of this line is the one transmitted to us in all modern editions, and in fact in all editions since the Second Folio itself, which was "corrected" in accordance with Q_2. Q_2 reads:

CLOWN: Why heere in Denmarke: I have been Sexten heere man and boy thirty yeeres.[14]

The discrepancy of readings seems vitally important, and yet, owing to a rather monumental oversight, has not even caused a controversy. What has happened is that the "sixteene" in the Folio has simply been considered either a variant spelling of "sexton" (to the amazing extent that the *Oxford English Dictionary* so lists it, and lists the *Hamlet* line as the sole source of the variant) or as, in Dover Wilson's words, a "slip, probably compositor's."[15]

At the very least I think I can point out that "sixteene" is not a variant spelling of "sexton," and that it is not a compositor's slip. I am quite certain, in fact, that the compositor of the First Folio meant to say with this line exactly what he did say (and what he presumed Shakespeare meant to say), that Hamlet was sixteen. That won't end the matter, of course, but it will form the first link in a chain of evidence which might help us to know what Shakespeare did mean.

In the first place, "sixteene" cannot simply be considered a variant spelling or mis-spelling of a word it resembles as little as "sexton." "Sexton" is not a difficult or unfamiliar word; its spelling had been regularized by the late sixteenth century, and it appears in the Folio five times, always spelled exactly as it is today. Just thirty speeches back, Hamlet speaks of a "sextons spade"; the compositor had no trouble with it that time. The word "sixteen," similarly, shows near perfect regularity in its Folio spellings: it appears there (omitting the present reference) twelve times, and is spelled "'sixteene" eleven of them, and "sixteen" once. If we were concerned with a matter of variant spelling, then the copy in error would almost have to be Q_2, for it is considerably easier to get "sexten" from "sixteen" (one letter changed and one dropped) than "sixteene" from "sexton," (two letters changed and two added). In fact, "sexten" is a known variant spelling of "sixteen," as listed in 1483 and 1549 references in the *Oxford English Dictionary*. Besides this, Q_2 was the more poorly spelled of the two versions.[16] If there is a spelling error of any kind, then, it is almost surely in the Quarto and not the Folio.[17]

A secondary piece of evidence buttresses this assertion, and that is concerned with the internal punctuation of the lines in question. The Quarto line has no commas or punctuation of any sort, but the Folio line has a comma after "heere," reading "I have been sixteene heere, man and Boy thirty yeares." The compositor of the preceding Folio line, it seems to me, would have been unlikely to have inserted (or retained from manuscript) that comma if he thought he was only spelling "sexton" some other way.

To do so would have mined the speaking sense of the sentence. He could, perhaps, have put in two commas (another after Boy) but he would not have put in just one, which would divide the two pieces of information he was trying to link. On the other hand, if the compositor assumed the line meant "I have been here for sixteen years, and alive for thirty," he would have placed the comma exactly where it appears. So unless the compositor of the Folio line made two unrelated and quite improbable errors— misreading "sexton" from the manuscript and adding a faulty comma—then we can be almost certain that he meant to say exactly what he did say, that Hamlet is sixteen.

We are now in the position of concluding that, if this were a matter of variant spelling, the Folio would be correct and the Quarto in error. But nothing indicates positively that it is a matter of spelling at all. We have only shown that the Folio compositor thought he knew what he was doing; we have not shown the Quarto compositor doing any less. In other words, they both could have looked at the handwritten sources they were working from, and come up with different interpretations of the manuscript; that is, the Folio compositor thought the word was "sixteen," and the Quarto compositor thought it was "sexton." Which one was right?

Again, tradition seems to hold with the Quarto. Although it is more sloppily spelled, and at first glance looks less polished than the later Folio text, the Quarto has been widely held as the more authoritative version for more than a hundred years. Dover Wilson's superb study of the text of *Hamlet* has been refined since its 1934 publication, but his conclusions relevant to this matter remain undisturbed.[18] Wilson finds that the F_1 compositor worked from a fair copy produced by a member of Shakespeare's company (probably an actor) from the original Globe Theatre prompt-book, and that Q_2 was set up directly by a meticulous but theatrically-unwise compositor directly from Shakespeare's own "autograph copy," the "foul papers." Wilson goes on to describe the men in question. The transcriber of F_1 was a man thoroughly familiar with the play, whose errors (and there were many) stemmed from his very knowledge of the play, which caused him to anticipate lines and paraphrase the text. His mind, apparently, was continually racing ahead of his tedious transcribing duties, and he filled in the play from memory rather than by painstakingly checking the original copy. By contrast the Q_2 compositor "appears as a plodder, reproducing his copy letter by letter and, when (as often) he cannot read a word, setting it up in a form which is as much like a typographical facsimile of the letters before him as he can make it."[19] To Wilson, this is reason to prefer the work of the Q_2 compositor; "he possessed neither understanding nor interest in the play . . . he was concerned merely with the letters he saw, or thought he saw, and his sole desire was to set them up in type as quickly as he could . . . if a passage did not make sense, that was the author's business."[20] But this same reasoning which makes Wilson prefer the Quarto should make us hold *against* the Quarto in this case.

The point of his findings should be that when variant readings in the two texts differ on style, form, diction, or meter, the Quarto reading should usually get the nod, but when the basic difference is one of sense, the Folio will more likely be correct. The reason is obvious; a person who knows the play would never confuse the meaning of "sixteen" and "sexton," the only person who would be so confused is someone who only saw the words as scrawls on a manuscript. If we examine the variant readings between the texts, we find that the known errors of the Folio are almost invariably matters of diction, meter, poetry, or eloquence; rarely of sense. Q_2, on the other hand, abounds in clearly demonstrable errors that are totally illogical. Thus in the Quarto we find Hamlet saying "these can devote me truly" (instead of "denote me truly"), "wary, stale, flat, and unprofitable" (instead of "weary, stale, flat, and unprofitable"), "seale-slaughter" (instead of "self-slaughter"), "why she should hang on him" (instead of "why she would hang on him"), "sallied flesh" (instead of "solid flesh"). The Folio errors, by contrast, are all sensible if weak substitutions: for example Horatio says "the cock, that is the trumpet to the day" (instead of "to the morn"), Marcellus says "no spirit can walk abroad" (instead of "no spirit dare stir abroad,") the Queen implores Hamlet to "cast thy nightly color off" (instead of "nighted color"), and Hamlet says, "I would not have your enemy say so" (instead of "I would not hear your enemy say so"). While these lines are drawn solely from the play's first two scenes, the principle applies throughout: that where the *sense* of the variant reading is in question, the Folio is more likely to be in tune with the author's intention. The actor who transcribed *Hamlet* for the Folio may have been no poet, but he knew what the play was about. As a recent critic has similarly deduced, "it now seems . . . likely . . . that the variants in F represent what was actually spoken on the stage."[21] I think we stand here with the first link in our chain; that the Folio is correct and the Quarto (and succeeding texts) in error, and that the intention of the clown's first line is to tell us that Hamlet is sixteen.

But immediately we are confronted with the next piece of evidence as to Hamlet's age, and it comes right on the heels of the first.

CLOWN: Heres a Scull now: this Scul, has laine in the earth three & twenty years. (F_1)

CLOWN: heer's a scull now hath lyen you i'th earth 23. yeeres. (Q_2)

And in both texts Hamlet exclaims how he knew Yorick, rode his back, and kissed his lips. How can we reconcile this with what has gone before? Though there seems to be a marked textual discrepancy in the spelling, wording, and punctuation of the two lines, the meaning seems to be identical in both: implicitly that Hamlet is about twenty-seven.

A route out of this dilemma is provided by the "bad" First Quarto of *Hamlet*. Unfortunately the sexton/sixteen line has no equivalent in the severely reduced text of the 1603 Q_1, but a variation of the Yorick dialogue does appear. Here is the relevant line:

CLOWN: Looke you, heres a scull hath bin here this dozen yeare

So, upon first reading of Q_1, we find that Yorick has been dead only twelve years, not twenty-three. And if Hamlet remembered him from about age four-the age when young children are generally carried about on servants' backs, and still young enough to be kissed on the lips—then again we find that Hamlet is about sixteen.

Admittedly this interpretation has a few difficulties. In the first place, it is not certain that the Clown is speaking of Yorick's skull at first, since thirteen lines come between the identification of a twelve-year-old skull and the lines addressed to Yorick's. Secondly, if this is Yorick's skull, that only sets a minimum age for Hamlet, and leaves open the possibility that Yorick lived on until Hamlet was, say, eighteen. I think these objections, however, can be met with fairly easily. For the first, the skull that is first brought up is certainly from a well-known corpse, or why would the clown remember the exact date of its interment? When Hamlet asks the name of the skull later on, he says "whose scull *was* this," not "is this," indicating that he is speaking of the skull they have already been discussing, instead of another one newly dug out of the ground. This, plus the lack of indication that any other skull has been exhumed, plus our awareness of normal dramatic economy, seems to indicate that we are speaking at the end of the scene of the same skull dug up at the beginning, and that that skull is Yorick's, and that he has been dead for twelve years.

As to Hamlet's age when Yorick dies, the assumption would obviously be that Hamlet's recollection of Yorick would be his last recollection rather than one at a middle point in Yorick's life. If the only memories Hamlet wishes to narrate about

Yorick were those of Hamlet's childhood, it may be presumed that is because he has no later memories of the old family retainer. Dramatic economy here too indicates Shakespeare would not be misleading his audience by having Hamlet recall Yorick at a rather arbitrary moment in Yorick's life, but rather at the final moments. I think that we can fairly assume that the transcriber, compositor, and, yes, the author of Q_1 definitely indicate that Yorick's death is twelve years past, that Hamlet's age at Yorick's death is about four, and that Hamlet is about sixteen. Primarily on this basis alone, a scholar has suggested that in Q_1 "the part of Hamlet has been altered for performance by a young man of nineteen,"[22] and a similar point of view will be discussed below.

But we are still left with a gigantic problem. All the texts seem to be clear as to their meaning on this line, and yet Q_1 is in flagrant contradiction to Q_2 and the Folio. In no way can we throw out Q_2 and F1 in favor of Q_1, of course, but I think it is possible to establish at least the partial legitimacy of the First Quarto to try and get a better picture of what is happening here, and to find out what Shakespeare actually intended. Scholars have long wrestled with the 1603 Quarto, and have suggested from time to time that it was a piracy, a stenographic report, a memorial reconstruction, a play of Kyd's, or an early draft of Shakespeare's play. A current opinion which has gained a share of scholarly acceptance indicates that it is a degenerated transcription of Shakespeare's first version of the play, greatly edited down for touring performances. In the words of Hardin Craig, "Q_1 is a version of Shakespeare's original play . . . a somewhat degenerated version of Shakespeare's earliest known play on the theme of Hamlet."[23] This view has been amplified and supported by Albert Weiner in *Hamlet, The First Quarto 1603*,[24] and while the findings of Craig and Weiner have been the subject of considerable controversy, they give weight to the opinion that Q_1 is in fact an invaluable guide to Shakespeare's primary vision of *Hamlet*. For all of its bewildering editing and cutting, Q_1 amazingly gets in or reports virtually all the action of the play, and all the necessary information for following that action; the sense and story of *Hamlet,* if not the grandeur, are intact. Editors today implicitly follow this reasoning when they use Q_1 readings to arbitrate between variances in the two "good" texts, and very occasionally even prefer Q_1. This reasoning gives credence to the suggestion that the Quarto's implication of Hamlet as sixteen is not an error but an indication of Shakespeare's original if not his realized intention.

When we turn to the sources of *Hamlet*, we find similar indications. The "Ur-Hamlet," certainly the prime source, has not survived, but the original novella has.

This is a tale by Belleforest, which appeared in his *Histoires Tragiques* in 1582; it was translated by Thomas Pavier and published in London as *The Hystorie of Hamblet* in 1608, about seven years after the play's public premiere. It is generally assumed that Shakespeare used the Belleforest as well as the "Ur-Hamlet"; either he read it in French, or in a draft of Pavier's (or someone else's) translation. Pavier's work certainly followed the play's production, because he incorporated some of Shakespeare's lines ("A rat! A rat!") into the story where they had not hitherto appeared.

In the Belleforest/Pavier story, Hamlet quite specifically appears as a juvenile: an only child at the mercy of tyrannical adults; even after killing the King he cries plaintively to the citizens, "take pitty of an orphan child, so abandoned of the world."[25] Earlier in the story he chides his mother, saying, "it is not the parte of a woman, much less a princesse, . . . thus to leave her deare child to fortune in the bloody and murtherous hands of a villain and traytor."[26] He is described no less than fourteen times in the text as a "young" man or a "youth." And most importantly, the first time he is mentioned in the story (after the notation of his birth) is when Fengon explains that Hamlet is "of such a mind that if he once attained to mans estate he would not long delay the time to revenge the death of his father."[27] Belleforest explicitly makes Hamlet a minor, and in fact bases the action of his novella on that fact; Pavier, writing after Shakespeare's play, makes no attempt to "correct" or change that implication.

At this point I should like to summarize these findings:

1. The 1582 French source, as well as its 1608 English translation, explicitly state that Hamlet has not yet "attained to man's estate, " and describes him rather as a "youth" and a "young man," and has him describe himself as his mother's "dear child."

2. All versions of Hamlet show the prince to be, particularly in the first four acts, "young," a "boy," "primy," and "of the younger sort," and, moreover, use these descriptions to suggest that he's too young to seriously think about marriage.

3. The 1603 Quarto, generally believed to be Shakespeare's first published version of the play, strongly suggests, through the clown's line, that Hamlet is about sixteen, and has absolutely no suggestions that he is a day older.

4. The 1623 Folio, generally understood in the case of this play to most closely reflect what was actually said on the stage indicates, through the clown's line, that Hamlet is precisely sixteen years old in the last act; however it then contradicts itself in the same seen by indicating that Hamlet knew and kissed a man (Yorick) who had been dead for twenty-three years.

5. Finally, the 1605 Quarto indicates that Hamlet is thirty years old (per the clown's line) and at least older than 23 (per the gravedigger's line). And it is the version that is, up to now, universally considered decisive.

But at best the evidence is ambiguous, and, I would argue, weighted in favor of establishing Hamlet's age not at thirty, which is ludicrous from a Renaissance point of view, but rather at the ripening age of sixteen.

How can we explain the remaining ambiguity? A case may be made that there has been an intentional change in the manuscript: that the date of Yorick's death has been deliberately pushed back eleven years for some reason, and that this change did not take place until after the play had been fully conceptualized and drafted by the author.

Shakespeare had no trouble being explicit about the age of his heroines. Juliet is thirteen, Marina fourteen, Miranda fifteen, Perdita sixteen. His young men, by contrast, are never given specific ages. Historically Prince Hal was sixteen at Shrewsbury, but Shakespeare never mentions this, and the tone of the play indicates he is somewhat older. There is an obvious reason: Shakespeare's heroines were played by child actors, and his male leads were played by "stars." Hamlet was played by Richard Burbage, who was 34 in 1601, and though hardly conceivable as a sixteen-year-old youth, was not to be denied the title role as the leading actor and heir apparent of his company. I think it reasonable to suggest Burbage's influence in pushing back the date of Yorick's death. Dover Wilson discusses thirteen lines (none in question in this essay) which he considers "Burbage's additions" to the F_1 text.[28] Burbage had the power, it seems, to do this; so rather than deciding that the Q_1 text was changed to accommodate a young actor, I suggest that the Q_2 text was changed to accommodate Burbage.[29] He would not have had to change the clown's line about "sixteene," because in the context, of a rapidly acted performance, the audience would not have time to collect all the evidence (which is spread across fifteen lines) to make the A=B, B=C, A=C deduction necessary to arrive at Hamlet's age. But the Q_1 inference that this man was kissing him on the lips only a dozen years ago would have been a different matter. I assume Shakespeare, as a loyal playwright, went along with the emendation, for it apparently went into his autograph copy that served as the basis for Q_2. The Burbage emendation-so I consider it-defies the sense, tone and imagery of the play, and is a concession to a peculiarity of Elizabethan staging which now should properly be dropped. I further think that the original concept of Shakespeare's that Hamlet is sixteen, can effectively be restored.

There are a multitude of critical directions that can be taken from the foregoing suggestions, but at this point I should like to limit myself to a purely personal speculation. Shakespeare had a son named Hamnet who was born in 1585, and who died in 1596. "Hamlet," is simply a variant spelling of "Hamnet." Hamnet would have been sixteen in 1601, which is generally considered the date of Hamlet's first public performance.

Traditionally, Shakespeare is considered to have performed the role of the Ghost in the premiere of Hamlet. If this were true, then the first Elizabethan audience would have witnessed the author "playing" the father of a sixteen-year-old boy named Hamlet—only in life it was the son who was a ghost, not the father. It would have been a chilling situation. Perhaps it may help to explain the general feeling, universally sensed but never provable, that Hamlet is Shakespeare's most personal play.

NOTES

1 Except where noted, quotations from *Hamlet* are taken from *The New Shakespeare Hamlet*, ed. John Dover Wilson (Cambridge: 1934).

2 Quotations from the First Quarto of *Hamlet* (Q1) are taken from the G. B. Harrison edition(New York: 1966), a facsimile of the copy in the British Museum. In quoting from the *Hamlet* texts, I have modernized the f/s and u/v typography, but otherwise retained the spelling, punctuation, and italicization.

3 Eduard and Otto Devrient, in H. H. Furness, *Hamlet Variorum* (Philadelphia: 1877), II, p. 346.

4 Minto, in Furness, II, p. 346.

5 *Hamlet and Revenge*, 2nd ed. (Stanford: 1971), p. 126.

6 (Copenhagen: 1924).

7 *Young Hamlet* (Aberdeen: 1950).

8 Blackstone, in Furness, I, 390.

9 Grant White, in Furness, I, 391.

10 "Neither Fat nor Thirty," *Shakespeare Quarterly*, 2 (1957), p. 298.

11 *Ibid.*

12 Quotations from the First Folio are taken from the facsimile edition of Helge Kokeritz (New Haven: 1954).

13 This is the conclusion reached by John Dover Wilson, *The Manuscript of Shakespeare's Hamlet* (Cambridge: 1934), hereafter cited as *M.S.H.* More recent studies have tended to confirm Wilson's findings.

14 Quotations from the Second Quarto are taken from the facsimile edition of the

Devonshire copy (San Marino, CA: 1964). The Devonshire copy itself is now in the Huntington Library, San Marino, California.

15 Wilson, *M.S.H.,* II, p. 345.

16 "The *Hamlet* of 1623 is, superficially at least, a clean piece of work; that is to say, it is well printed. The *Hamlet* of 1605, on the other hand, so teems with misprints, with strange spellings, with missing letters, and with omitted words, lines and passages, that perusal of a single page is likely to inspire the uninitiated with distaste and distrust." John Dover Wilson, *M.S.H.,* I, p. 88.

17 Did they sound alike? Helge Kokeritz has suggested that "sexton" and "sixteen" were homonymic puns, and sounded alike in the seventeenth century (*Shakespeare's Pronunciation,* New Haven, CT: 1953, pp. 144-45). However this suggestion is based entirely on the presumption of a misspelling in the Folio at precisely the line in question, and I believe it to be in error. Elsewhere (pp. 185, 190, 212, 256) Kokeritz shows that the vowels in both words were ordinarily pronounced about as they are today, and although "eh" could occasionally be widened to "ih," Kokeritz gives no phonological instances of the schwa (the second vowel in "sexton") being brought forward as "ee" as in "sixteen."

18 The refinements in Wilson's theories have been to elucidate the work of various compositors within each edition of the play, instead of assuming the work was of an individual man in each case. The overall comparison of the texts, however, remains intact. See articles by Harold Jenkins, Fredson Bowers, and John Russell Brown in *Studies in Bibliography* (1955), pp. 17-40; Alice Walker, *Textual Problems in the First Folio* (London: 1953); and F. P. Wilson and Helen Gardner, *Shakespeare and the New Bibliography* (Oxford: 1970).

19 *M.S.H.,* I, p. 100.

20 *M.S.H.,* I, pp. 100-201.

21 Harold Jenkins, "Playhouse Interpolations of the Folio Text of *Hamlet,*" *Studies in Bibliography,* 13 (1960), p. 46. I think this reasoning should put the final nail in the coffin of Q$_2$'s "sallied" flesh.

22 R. Compton Rhodes, *Shakespeare's First Folio,* quoted in G.B. Harrison, ed., *The Tragicall Historie of Hamlet,* 1603 (New York: 1966), p. xii.

23 *A New Look at Shakespeare's Quartos* (Stanford: 1961).

24 (New York, 1962).

25 In Sir Israel Gollancz, *The Sources of Hamlet* (New York: 1967), p. 277.

26 *Ibid.,* p. 213.

27 *Ibid.*, p. 193.

28 *M.S.H.* "Burbage's additions to his part," I, pp. 77-82.

29 In making that change, Burbage created an additional problem for another actor—the
Clown. According to my interpretation, the Clown would be 30; stage tradition has
presented our age with a gravedigger further on in years. But the role, after all, was created almost certainly by Robert Armin, who was about 33 at the time, and seemed to
look younger than he was, according to Baldwin, *Organization and Personnel of the
Shakespearean Company* (Princeton: 1927).

CHAPTER

11 Coming of Age in Elsinore

In the previous chapter I report bibliographic material discrediting the Gravedigger's apparent evidence that Hamlet is thirty years old, providing evidence suggesting that Shakespeare meant Hamlet to be a boy of sixteen. If correct, the implications of this new reading would be quite striking, both in terms of the interpretation of the play's basic story, and in terms of the play's metadramatic structure. Even if incorrect, a youthful Hamlet seems at the heart of Shakespeare's play.

And so it happened that at the University of California at Irvine, in February 1986, I staged a *Hamlet* with a slight (135 pound), youthful, literally teenage (nineteen) undergraduate actor, Paul Lovely, in the title role, playing opposite two professional actors of paternal age, substantial in height and girth, in the father and stepfather (Ghost and Claudius) roles, and with a graduate actress, herself the mother of a preteen boy, as Gertrude.

The production process was unusually detailed. The play was performed virtually uncut, and ran nearly four-and-a-half hours with two intermissions. The rehearsal period was 14 weeks long with five-hour nightly rehearsals; the first five weeks of rehearsal took place in a small cleared classroom, and were devoted to fairly exhaustive discussions and playing with various possibilities of movements, actions, property business, and improvisations. Although the basic setting had been designed, no staging was attempted for the first 125 hours of rehearsal. The play was set in a Denmark closely resembling Hohenzollern Germany, where duelling, hunting, and beer drinking were popular royal entertainments, and where militarism was fundamental to student and political life. The setting could be described as an abandoned 19th century munitions factory, with rusty steel catwalks, four steel staircases (two circular), and seemingly steam-operated sliding doors which operated (seemingly) by pull chains. The setting was littered with industrial waste and reminiscent of a prison (Denmark is

Originally published in *On Stage Studies*, Summer 1987

"*Oh, that this too too solid flesh would melt.*" Hamlet (Paul Lovely) in his military school uniform banded with a black mourning sash, contemplates the unweeded garden.

"*We beseech you, bend you to remain/Here in the cheer and comfort of our eye,/Our chiefest courtier, cousin, and our son.*" Claudius, played by Dudley Knight, wickedly kneels as he beseeches his new step-son, thereby undermining Hamlet's rebellious teenage sarcasm. Hamlet has no choice but to yield, though to his mother (played by Cynthia Blaise) rather than to his uncle.

one, says Hamlet); it also had a jungle-gym (monkey bars) quality, however, which gave rise to lots of youthful running, climbing, swinging around poles, and general playfulness. An actual swing hung from one of the catwalks; it was from the swing that Hamlet would begin his "too too solid flesh" soliloquy. Hamlet and his school friends (Horatio, Marcellus, Rosencrantz, Guildenstern) wore military school uniforms. The precise period was left deliberately fuzzy, however, so that the play's psychological and political levels were not buried under mere historicity, even of an updated sort, and so that social and familial relationships could be largely seen in ahistorical (i.e., universal) terms. The design team, Douglas Scott Goheen (scenery), Chuck Goheen (costumes), and Cameron Harvey (lighting) had worked together with me many times, and we all participated collaboratively on these matters in many of the exploratory rehearsals and discussions.

Of course the question that preoccupied us was the matter Hamlet's "delay"; which is to say, "Why doesn't Hamlet avenge his father's death right away?" That this question has been asked for centuries does not make it any less interesting; it is really just another way of asking "what does Hamlet do during the course of the play?" There are two main contexts in which answers to this question may be pursued: a psychological context, where we consider the characters to be people, and a structural context, where we consider the characters to be dramatic integers. Thus the sorts of answers one is used to finding are from seemingly unrelated concerns: either "Hamlet delays because he has a mother fixation" (psychological context) or "Hamlet delays because if he didn't there would be no play" (structural context). I was hoping to relate these concerns, to address the question in both contexts simultaneously, and to come up with a staging which produced an integrated response.[1]

To me, the psychological problem is that Hamlet has been more or less emasculated by Claudius, "the cutpurse of the empire," who has not only "popped in between [Hamlet's] election and [his] hopes," but who has interceded between Hamlet's mother and her son, and assumed the role of surrogate father to the adolescent Prince. Hamlet suffers, consequently, from an acutely arrested male development. This problem becomes a bit more obvious if we believe that Hamlet is only 16 years old when he returns to Elsinore, where he finds his uncle in his father's throne, in his father's bed, and fully engaged carrying out his father's role. Although psychological inquiry into the play has generally centered on the Prince's Oedipal fixations on Gertrude, I believe the relations between sons and fathers, and on the natural male succession to manhood, is far more central to Shakespeare's concern here. "Death of fathers" is reason's "common theme," says Claudius. So, if anything, Hamlet has a father—not a mother—fixation.[2]

Hamlet's dramatic path is to grow into his father's role: that Shakespeare named him with his father's name (apparently an invention: in Belleforest they are named Ambleth [son] and Horvendile [father]) only makes that more explicit. But who was Hamlet's father? "A goodly King," says Horatio. "A *man*," corrects Hamlet.[3]

To the world, the late King was a celebrated figure; to his son, he was, beneath idealized, god-like trappings, simply (but crucially) a man: the very symbol of manhood. "Hyperion's curls, the front of Jove himself, an eye like Mars, . . . a station like the herald Mercury . . . " these divine attributes only added up, Hamlet says, to "a combination and a form indeed where every god did seem to set his seal to give the world assurance of a man." It is this goal of manhood to which Hamlet aspires: but how can he achieve it? Hamlet's sole role model is gone. His mother is suspect. His schoolfriends—some of them at least—are commissioned spies. His girlfriend acts her father's orders. He is forbidden to return to school. He sees ghosts. How does a sensitive teenage boy grow into manhood under these circumstances? Shakespeare takes five acts to answer that question, and so did we.

Shakespeare traces Hamlet's quest for manhood through images of penile erection: Hamlet measures his powers throughout the play on a variety of phallic continuums: limp to stiff, dull to sharp, short to long, and impotent to ejaculatory. On hearing the Ghost's accusations for the first time, Hamlet's immediate reaction is to urge his body towards erectility:

> Hold, hold, my heart
> And you, my sinews, grow not instant old
> But bear me stiffly up.

Sinew stiffness as a symbol of manliness is reminiscent of Henry the Fifth's battle cry: "stiffen the sinews, summon up the blood"—and of Claudius's later boast to Laertes that his reasons, though they "perhaps seem much unsinewed, yet to me they're strong."

Stiffness implies the ability to penetrate; so does sharpness. Claudius continues to Laertes, "You must not think that we are made of stuff so flat and dull that we can let our beard be shook." Yet Hamlet, by contrast, is overwhelmed by his dullness, flatness, feebleness, and infirmity. "Weary, stale, flat and unprofitable" is his world. "A dull and

muddy-mettled rascal," he calls himself. " My dull revenge," he expostulates. The
Ghost charges Hamlet: "duller shouldst thou be than the fat weed that roots itself in
ease on Lethe wharf[4] wouldst thou not stir in this ("Lethe," according to the Oxford
English Dictionary, connotes "flaccidity,") and the Ghost returns to "whet" (i.e.,
sharpen) Hamlet's "almost blunted purpose." By contrast, Laertes is urged not to "dull
thy palm," and not to do that which will "dulleth edge of husbandry." Laertes is sharp,
and Fortinbras is certainly stiffly up. Fortinbras, "strong-of-arm" by name, is of "unim-
proved mettle" (homonymic with metal), and has "sharked up" an army somewhere "in
the skirts of Norway." A clearly developed potency is implied for all the play's male
protagonists, save the Prince, and that was exemplified by the UCI casting: a brilliantly vigorous and flashy graduate actor as Laertes, an Adonis-like Icelandic six-footer as
Fortinbras, and a towering, sensual, powerful, mature professional actor (Dudley
Knight) as Claudius.

   Hamlet, by contrast, is seen as virginal, sexually prepubescent, almost childlike. In
this Shakespeare clearly differs from Belleforest, in whose novella the Hamlet prototype gleefully copulates with "Ophelia" in the forest, prior to killing "Claudius." In
Hamlet, however, the Prince presumably dies a virgin (Ophelia explicitly does so), and
Hamlet's sexual acts are restricted to sublimating tirades: "Get thee to a nunnery,"
(during which, at Irvine, Hamlet stamped repeatedly on the steel runway above
Ophelia's head, adolescence in extremis). Hamlet's only sexual acts are his nocturnal
emissions (wet dreams):

Yet I,
A dull and muddy-mettled rascal, peak
Like John-a-dreams, unpregnant of my cause,
And can say nothing.

   Unsharp, unfirm, unable to impregnate, coming at the wrong time, Hamlet accus-
es himself of being womanish, not manly: a "whore," a "drab," a "scullion" (washer-
woman).[5] He refers to himself as an "arrant knave," and "so poor a man as Hamlet."
The Devil, on the other hand, he finds "potent," and may succeed out of "my weak-
ness." Others recognize Hamlet's flaccidity. Polonius says that Hamlet's tenders are
"not sterling" (e.g., not like silver, not hard, as metal) and Laertes similarly says that
Hamlet "may not . . . carve for himself." Claudius calls his grief "unmanly." When
Hamlet says to Claudius "your worm is your only emperor," Hamlet clearly identifies

with the "politic worms," as those that live in Lethe wharf, that insinuate themselves, limply, like Hamlet, into a sea of troubles.

Hamlet is not necessarily impotent, at the physical level, or physically dysfunctional; but he is psychologicly blocked. He is simply not ready to do what needs to be done. It is the time which is out of joint, and therefore it is readiness which is lacking—the readiness which will, eventually, be "all." When Hamlet will be ready, he will assume his manly role; he will act through forthright strength rather than adolescent sarcasm or wormlike insinuation; he will be able to carve for himself. The phallic imagery resolves itself in swords and swordplay.

The so-called first court scene (I.ii) at UCI began with a staged ceremonial duel—between the yet unintroduced Laertes and a duelling master. We used Schlager duelling, which was peculiar to German student societies: Schlager duellists come together in a close circle, and, wearing cloth helmets and eye goggles, seek to inflict facial wounds. In the scene, Claudius, Gertrude, and the court drink beer and cheer the competitors. Hamlet sulks unnoticed at the corner of the action. He is uncomfortable with swords, and, as he soon says, he does not set the value of his life at a "pin's fee." Later he will compare himself to a "little organ," a pipe-like recorder:

> You would play upon me, you would seem to know my stops . . . and there is much music, excellent voice, in this little organ, yet cannot you make it speak. 'Sblood, do you think I am easier to be played on than a pipe?

The recorder is hardly the kind of organ Laertes has in mind when he demands of Claudius "that I might be the organ" of Hamlet's death, or the organ Hamlet refers to when he says that "murder, though it have no tongue, will speak with a most miraculous organ." That organ—for murder and for revenge—is clearly a sword: a stage property which, like the recorder, has obvious phallic connotations. Yet Hamlet is not now ready to use a sword.

Hamlet's first actual use of a sword is masturbatory rather than martial:

> Swear't . . . Upon my sword . . . Indeed, upon my sword, indeed . . . Swear by my sword . . . Come hither gentlemen, and lay your hands again upon my sword. Swear by my sword.

Hamlet's sword in the first act is essentially an icon for swearing by, and for the laying on of hands. Traditional business has Hamlet turning the sword hilt upwards, making it into a crucifix, a symbol of nonresistance to evil. At UCI the sword was used to break skin, and to share in a blood pact; the swordplay in the fifth scene then was a first step towards Hamlet's maturation.

Still, Hamlet is functionally unarmed at the beginning of the play. This in striking contrast to the ghost, who arrives, we are told repeatedly, "armed at point . . . armed in complete steel." Shakespeare courts redundancy here. "Armed say you?" Hamlet asks; "Armed, my lord," he hears. And one more time, perhaps in agony: "My father's spirit, in arms?" Yes. But Hamlet still pivots on his own decision, "whether to take up arms." And his first answer is no. "I will speak daggers to her but use none." He will commit suicide, if need be, "with a bare bodkin," with a woman's sewing needle. Such is the instrument of a young man who sets his life at a pin's fee.

Hamlet's reluctance to use arms was played at Irvine as phobic; specifically belanophobic, which describes a documented mental illness: the irrational fear of swords. His fear is that his sword will fail him at the crucial moment: a fear we actually staged in the play-within-the play of Dido and Aeneas, an excerpt of which Hamlet and the Players present in Act II.[6] Hamlet begins by giving the speech in Dido that he "chiefly loved," a speech where the Trojan Pyrrhus, "tricked with blood of fathers," seeks to kill "the unnerved father" Priam. But Hamlet breaks off the speech, begging the First Player to continue. At Irvine, other players took costumes and props from their trunk, and, mounting the upper stage, mimed the swordplay as the First Player spoke:

Anon he [Pyrrhus] finds him [Priam,]
Striking too short at Greeks. His antique sword
Rebellious to his arms, lies where it falls:
Repugnant to command.

Hamlet, below, mimed pulling his own sword, and re-enacted Priam's sword-dropping action, along with the actor above. Then Hamlet assumed Pyrrhus' part, as the First Player described Pyrrus' assault on the "old Grandsire Priam."

For lo! His sword
Which was declining on the milky head
Of reverent Priam, seemed i' the air to stick.

Hamlet's sword, as Pyrrhus', seems i'the air to stick; he too is a painted tyrant.

And Hamlet, echoing the player above, found his own sword paralyzed in the air above his head—just as it would later appear in the play in the King's closet.

> So as a painted tyrant Pyrrhus stood,
> And like a neutral to his will and matter,
> Did nothing.

And Hamlet knows that he too is like a painted revenger, whose acts do not cohere with his words or thoughts. But, unlike Hamlet (at this point), Pyrrhus' inaction is only a "pause," after which:

> Aroused vengeance sets him new a-work;
> And never did the Cyclop's hammers fall
> On Mars's armor, forged for proof eterne,
> With less remorse than Pyrrhus' bleeding sword
> Now falls on Priam.

And as the Player's Pyrrhus' sword fell on the Player Priam, so Hamlet's mimed sword fell on the bare stage together with Hamlet's horrible battle cry: a cry which no one had heard before. It is a cry, and an emotional explosion, and a violent (mimed) use of a violent weapon which makes Polonius exceptionally nervous; Polonius correctly reads the action as a rehearsal for a future act: perhaps the running through of an aged councilor behind an arras or something like that. Polonius tries to call off the recitation: "This is too long." But Hamlet will drive the play (*Dido*) and the play (*Hamlet*) forward.

In the *Dido* scene, Hamlet discovers three things. First, he sees that the act of playing can help him connect his feelings to his actions, and his actions to his words (it is for this reason that he will later insist that the actors "suit the action to the word, the word to the action").

Second, he learns how to use a sword in heat; the act of acting Priam's killer will help him connect his murderous instincts to his physical capability. Acting will train his psychomotor responses.

Third, he sees that playing a hero will help him learn how to become a hero, become a king. Swordplaying can be rehearsed by stage playing; so can hero playing. "He that plays the King shall be welcome," he says, for Hamlet can learn how to be a king by first learning how to *play* a king. This theme is prominent in the subtext of

SECTION TWO: *On Plays*

the ensuing Hecuba speech, for while the soliloquy is largely self-deprecatory, it has a positive purpose: Hamlet will find his true power in playing and will undermine the Claudian conspiracy (as well as test the Ghost's legitimacy) by putting on a play. This is, as we often forget, the soliloquy that ends "The play's the thing." Hamlet begins the speech a victim, and ends it a producer.

Hamlet staged the play *The Murder of Gonzago* himself, at Irvine; handing out programs, seating the audience, advising the Players (from the back of the real "house," as the Players rehearsed onstage the new dialogue he had given them), and, at the entrance of Lucianus, operating the followspots during the climax of the *Gonzago* performance. When Hamlet tells Claudius of the murderer getting the love of Gonzago's wife, he turned his followspot on Claudius and Gertrude, causing them to rise. Hamlet's "Frightened by false fire" became a reference to the light of the followspot, and Claudius' "give me some light" and Polonius' "Lights, lights, lights" were demands for "houselights" to replace the focused spotlight that Hamlet was wielding against them like a rapier.

In the King's closet, Hamlet draws his sword but doesn't kill Claudius. It is important that there be something more than just Hamlet's own explanation of this, if Hamlet (and *Hamlet)* is to have a psychological dimension. The King's closet was an upstairs "office" at UCI, with a balcony in front; at Hamlet's entrance the King had just dismissed Rosencrantz and Guildenstern, and, when telling them "Arm you," had given them revolvers from his desk drawer; then the King stepped out on the balcony and knelt to pray. Hamlet appeared beneath, seeing his stepfather through the open metal grating of the balcony above. Silently climbing the stairs, Hamlet crept behind Claudius, into the open "office," and aimed his sword for the kill. But of course he didn't kill. At this point Hamlet has precisely re-enacted the armed Pyrrhus over the kneeling Priam he had rehearsed before, (Claudius' "office" was the same space used for the Dido mime), and like Pyrrhus, Hamlet found his sword "seemed i'the air to stick." Hamlet's primal fantasy had struck; his sword, like Priam's, had proven repugnant to command, and Hamlet was forced instead to rationalize. His self-command to "do't" had become merely a suggestion to be "scanned," i.e., put into words, even into verse. Words, words, words. Hamlet remained still a painted tyrant.

It is precisely out of the overwhelming frustration of the King's closet scene that Hamlet, a few moments later, stabs through the bulge in the Queen's arras—with the nonhuman and faraway cry, "How now! A rat! Dead for a ducat, Dead!" ("Out, out, thou strumpet Fortune!" Pyrrhus yelled at Priam's corpse in Dido). At Irvine, Hamlet pulled down the entire arras, revealing Polonius' bloody corpse. A melodramatic action which was an acting out that proved, for the young prince, a psychological necessity, an antiphobic unblocking, a rehearsal of Hamlet's use of primal weaponry.

Hamlet's killing of Polonius may be a tactical mistake, but for the young Prince it is a psychological breakthrough. To hark back to Belleforest, Hamlet is beginning to come to man's estate. Though he will still speak daggers and use none to his mother, partially in response to the Ghost's command, he is achieving manly readiness. "How dangerous that this man goes loose," says Claudius at his next appearance; it is the first time in the play that Hamlet is referred to as an adult.

By the last act, Hamlet's "little organ" has come of age. "It is I, Hamlet the Dane," the Prince boldly cries as he leaps into Ophelia's grave, and his identity, maturity, and assumption of adult self-sufficiency, as well as his father's name and "title," is complete.

The completion is shown, by Shakespeare, in the sword/dagger imagery:

OSRIC: You are not ignorant of what excellence Laertes is—
HAMLET: I dare not confess that, lest I should compare with him in excellence, but to know a man were to know himself.
OSRIC: I mean, sir, for his weapon . . .
HAMLET: What's his weapon?
OSRIC: Rapier and dagger.
HAMLET: That's two of his weapons. But well.

Excellence = manhood = weaponry is the equation here, and weapons are both large and small. Large and small weapons are both the implements of the duel (rapier and dagger) and the winner's prize (rapiers and poignards), but Hamlet, by the Fifth Act, knows he can compete in such terms. He can "match" his rival.

CLAUDIUS (to Laertes): . . . for your rapier, most especial, [Lamord] cried out, 'twould be a slight indeed if one could match you.
. . . [And] this report . . .
Did Hamlet so envenom with his envy
That he could nothing do but wish and beg
Your sudden coming o'er to play with you.

So these two rivals are to be matched and played, weapon to weapon. In dialogue reminiscent of the locker room, Hamlet and Laertes compare their "weapons" for weight and length:

HAMLET: I'll be your foil, Laertes . . .
LAERTES: You mock me, sir.
HAMLET: No, by this hand . . .
. . . This [foil] is too heavy; let me see another.
LAERTES: This likes me well. These foils have all a length?

This is to be a duel of manhood. Both rivals spurn any latent femininity. Laertes suppresses his tears, telling Claudius, "when these are gone, the woman will be out." And Hamlet tries to throw aside "such gaingiving as would perhaps trouble a woman." The main plot yields to sexual innuendo and badinage:

HAMLET: You do but dally.
I pray you pass with your best violence.
I am afeard you make a wanton of me.

A suggestion of sexual connotation may be spurious in "pass," but it is explicit in "dally" and "wanton"; what is posited is that Hamlet sees this duel as his sexual coming out; the world shall see his sinews stiffly up, his grief manly, his tenders sterling, his purpose whetted, his weapon no pin nor a bodkin, his peaking not like John-a-dreams, but rather a climactic assault against his sea of troubles. That Shakespeare poses this coming of age in sexual terms should not be surprising; in the usual case, in which boys do not find their fathers assassinated during spring vacation, the coming of age process is primarily if not entirely sexual.

The duel culminates in a symbolic orgasm and ejaculation. Shakespeare denotes this by an extraordinary repetition of the word "come," which takes on totemic implications and may remind modern audiences of a famous monologue of Lenny Bruce. Hamlet's envy of Laertes' weapon makes the Prince "wish and beg" his rival's "sudden coming (o'er to play with you,)" and his response that he avoid the duel by declaring himself "not fit" is his famous statement of fatality:

If it be now, 'tis not to come; if it be not to come, it will be now; if it be not now, yet it will come.

The duel proceeds:

KING: Come, Hamlet, come, and take this hand from me . . .
HAMLET: Give us the foils, come on.
LAERTES: Come, one for me . . .
KING: Come, begin . . .
HAMLET: Come on sir.
LAERTES: Come, my lord . . .
HAMLET: Come . . . Another hit, what say you?
QUEEN: Come, let me wipe thy face . . .
HAMLET: Come for the third, Laertes . . .
LAERTES: Say you so? Come on . . .
HAMLET: Nay, come—again!

We have, but do not need, Eric Partridge's authority that "come" has the orgasmic connotation in Shakespeare as it does today, but such evidence is right in the text of *Hamlet* itself, where Ophelia's "Young men will do't if they come to't. By cock they are to blame" is explicitly associated with her "tumbled" maid. And Ophelia's song reinforces this metaphor:

And will 'a not come again?
And will 'a not come again?
No, no, he is dead;
Go to thy deathbed;
He never will come again.

Ophelia dies wrapped in a garland of "long purples, that liberal shepherds give a grosser name, but our cold maids do dead men's fingers call them." The grosser names are presumably "dead men's dicks," or something like that, associating sexuality with the dead that cannot "come" again.

The duel between Hamlet and Laertes concludes, of course, with liquid penetration (the unctioned swordpoint), and the double killing of Claudius, first with the sword, and then with the poisoned drink, emphasizes its orgasmic nature: intromission followed by insemination. "Is thy union here?" Hamlet shouts at the dying Claudius. This is not just a killing, it is "a consummation devoutly to be wished." The consummation is a union, one far stronger than that between Claudius and his imperial jointress; it is a union between Hamlet and his manhood; a union between the past and the future. The time is no longer out of joint, and the seeds are planted for a new union in Denmark.[7]

II

That Hamlet, a character in a play, achieves his goal through the intercession of players, and through the behavior of playing, calls for some special attention.[8] Hamlet's familiarity with plays and players, his fascination with theatrical metaphor, and the metadramatic structure of *Hamlet* (a play whose plot turns, in part, on the presentation of two other plays) are indices to a theatricalist expression. But the confluence of the theatricalist or metadramatic structure with the coming-of-age psychological process provides a unifying, if occasionally paradoxical, set of associations, which we tried to bring into focus at the Irvine production.

Popular usage defines "play" and "playing" as children's activities: thus Laertes' wish for Hamlet's "coming o'er to play"—out of context—has a distinctly juvenile air. The play's juxtaposition of game playing (swordplay) and theatrical playing (wordplay) only elaborates the youthfulness of play (within a play.)

The text of *Hamlet*, however, suggests that playing, at least dramatic playing, is strictly a grownup affair. Hamlet, I feel, makes this explicit in his opening scene; first with his highly adolescent wordplay to the King ("more than kin," "too much i'the sun"), and in his first speech to the Queen:

Seems, madam, Nay, it is. I know not 'seems.'
'Tis not alone my inky cloak, good mother,
Nor customary suits of solemn black,
Nor windy suspiration of forced breath,
No, nor the fruitful river in the eye,
Nor the dejected 'havior of the visage,
Together with all forms, moods, shapes of grief,
That can denote me truly. These indeed seem,
For they are the actions that a man might play.

But I have that within which passeth show—
These but the trappings and the suits of woe.

Hamlet's speech is, of course, an ironic attack on "acting" in daily life: the hypo-critical posturing, costuming, and external putting into "forms, moods [and] shapes" of what is, to the prince, "me truly." These self-manipulations are "actions that a man might play," says Hamlet, "but *I*" [i.e. not being a man] "have that within which pas-seth [a] show." I will not seem, I will not put on a show, I will not act.

But, of course, Hamlet is acting when he says this. For only 80 lines later he will lament "But break my heart, for I must hold my tongue." Hamlet will indeed "seem," and for the next four acts he will work to suppress "that within" in favor of putting on a show: windy suspirations to Ophelia, fruitful rivers to his mother, and dejected 'hav-iors to Polonius. "My tongue and soul in this be hypocrites," he says before visiting his mother, using the ancient Greek word for "actor." And he proselytizes his mother to this hypocrisy: "Assume a virtue if you have it not." Hamlet is hardly a paragon of nat-ural behavior or pre-Stanislavskian honesty. "I am indifferent honest," Hamlet tells Ophelia, and he is, in this instance, telling the truth.

Hamlet knows "seeming" well enough; what he doesn't understand is acting. So he approaches the art of acting—and, quite naturally, he approaches it through the (semantically) middle ground of "playing." His speeches, while representing a sort of child's play in the opening banter with Claudius, are all rehearsals for future acts.

Hamlet's first playing efforts are pathetic. "I am ill at these numbers," he writes Ophelia. His "antic disposition" is a tactical disaster. Whereas in the Belleforest novella Ambleth's pretended insanity had successfully diverted the King, Hamlet's feigned madness in Shakespeare's play only alarms the court and brings in the spies. Clearly, Hamlet needs tutors—and they arrive providentially in the persons of Players.

Shakespeare's invention of the Players provides Hamlet with his role models.[9] They are, as Hamlet greets them, his "masters." "You are welcome; masters, welcome all . . . Masters, you are all welcome," says the Prince. And, particularly, "He that plays the King shall be welcome." For it is the Player King who will show Hamlet how to play a King, so that Hamlet can then act as a King—both in the theatrical and nontheatrical sense.

Hamlet's fascination with the Players centers on their developing maturity. The Player who plays the King has grown into manhood:

HAMLET: O, old friend, why thy face is valenced since I saw thee last. Com'st thou to beard me in Denmark?

Do you come, in other words, to make a man of me here? Beards represent manliness: Claudius will not let his beard be shook. The boy actor, of course, has no beard, but he is quickly growing, and is a chopine (shoe, that is, foot) taller than before; Hamlet jokes that he will soon outgrow his female roles ("Pray God your voice . . . be not cracked.")—a growing up and out that Hamlet will, conversely, seek for himself.

Hamlet's interest extends to boy players in general; boys whose popularity is so great that they threaten to run adult theatres off the boards, boys who thereby "exclaim against their own succession." Any boy failing to achieve his true succession, particularly by his own deeds or lack of deeds, would, of course, fascinate a young Prince Hamlet. "Many wearing rapiers are afraid of goosequills," Rosencrantz reports: adult actors, represented by swords (Hamlet had earlier inquired as to whether the adult Players were "rusty") are frightened by boy actors, represented by goosequills (pins, bodkins). "Do the boys carry it away?" asks Hamlet in astonishment. "Aye, that they do, my lord—Hercules and his load too," Rosencrantz replies. This is a multiple reference. Hercules is the symbol of Shakespeare's Globe Theatre, but Hercules is also Hamlet's idol—one Hamlet has despaired of living up to. "No more like my father than I to Hercules," he says disparagingly of Claudius—and of himself. But even boy players have this Herculean power. They can defeat the older actors (take over the Globe) and stand up to their fathers. Hamlet will learn from them. The "boy players" scene, revealing a peculiarly contemporary theatre problem in Shakespeare's London, is almost always dropped from *Hamlet* productions as digressive, but it should be clear by now that far from digressing, Shakespeare is linking major lines in the play's thematic development with its structural presentation, and placing the coming-of-age psychological process into a theatrical (and theatricalist) context.

The *Dido and Aeneas* presentation, which was fully staged in mime at UCI, gives Hamlet his first chance to act: we placed him atop a circular staircase where one of the everpresent guards put a followspot on him as he spoke. Our Hamlet stumbled a bit at first (Shakespeare has him begin the Speech twice), but then reached a splendid melodramatic intensity and eloquence on "blood of fathers, mothers, daughters, sons." In the UCI production, we had not syllabalized metrical "eds" at the ends of words ordinarily unaccented in normal speaking (thus pronouncing "O curst spite" rather than "O curs-ed spite"); however in the play-within-a-play scenes we put them back: a satisfying way of making the play itself seem "real" in contrast to the theatrical presentations within the play. This also had the benefit of raising Hamlet to a feverish and highly theatrical pitch on "That lend a tyrannous and a damn-ed light," and brought his speech to a stunningly effective climax: at which everyone on stage stood momentarily in shock, a silence finally broken by the Player's sudden and enthusiastic applause, in which Polonius, Rosencrantz, and Guildenstern joined with true admiration. Hamlet was beginning to learn how to act.

The First Player takes over and continues the acting lesson, while, as described above, "Priam" and "Pyrrhus" mime the action above, and Hamlet shadows the role of Pyrrhus below. The boy actor grabs a robe from the trunk and mounts the stage to mime Hecuba, writhing at the sight of Pyrrhus "mincing with his sword her husband's limbs," as Hamlet mimics—and reacts to this primal scene.

Afterwards, in the Hecuba soliloquy, Hamlet analyzes what has just transpired.

Is it not monstrous that this player here
But in a fiction, in a dream of passion
Could force his soul so to his own conceit
That from her working all his visage wanned,
Tears in his eyes, distraction in's aspect,
A broken voice, and his whole function suiting
With forms to his conceit?

It is just what Hamlet repudiated in his "seems" speech: dejected behaviors; fruitful rivers; forced breath; forms, moods, and shapes of grief. Yes, Hamlet concludes, it remains monstrous. But Hamlet wrestles with his antitheatrical prejudice, and begins to rehearse his upcoming role:

Bloody, bawdy villain!
Remorseless, treacherous, lecherous, kindless, villain!
O vengeance!

But this is mere ranting, Hamlet decides: a feminine ("like a whore . . . a very drab, a scullion"), not a masculine form of acting. And so *Hamlet* turns into an acting class; but not acting merely from the point of view of dramaturgy, rather acting on a higher level, acting from the point of view of how to "make men."

O there be players that I have seen play . . . that neither having th'accent of . . . Christian, pagan, nor man, have so strutted and bellowed that I have thought some of Nature's journeymen had made men, and not made them well, they imitated humanity so abominably.

Hamlet argues for a human and a manly style, unaffected by stage ostentation and periwigs. While this may seem refreshingly modern today, we must note that it implies an external, not an internal technique, and emphasizes physical means of characterization (accent, gait, vocal delivery) rather than inner psychology or emotions.

Indeed, Hamlet even suggests that external "acting" will bring about appropriate internal feelings: sort of a cognitive dissonance theory of acting ("Do the act, the feeling will follow," is a common, modern phrasing of this concept.) When suggesting that his mother "assume a virtue if you have it not," Hamlet argues that if she repeatedly refuses to go to Claudius' bed, even though she may want to, she will soon come not to want to, for "use almost can change the stamp of nature, and either [curb] the devil, or throw him out with wondrous potency."[10] Thus the very stamp of nature," or "that within which passeth show," can be modified by "assumed" or simulated feelings, and these feelings can develop, in time, a "wondrous potency." Thus Hamlet plans to gain his virility, and through that his destiny, by acting.

Hamlet learns his craft, and produces his play. "The play's the thing wherein I'll catch the conscience of the King," he says, but what King? Claudius, of course, but also the King that Hamlet will become; it is through the play that he receives his own conscience, and his own power. It is through playing he will discover himself. At Irvine, as noted, Hamlet operated the followspots: he also recited the stage directions for the dumb show as it was mimed by the actors on stage: he was critically involved at every level of the Player's productions.

"I am set naked on your kingdom," writes Hamlet to Claudius on his return to Denmark in the final act, and with this letter Hamlet renounces not only the inky cloak, but costume altogether, as well as Polonius' claim that "apparel oft proclaims the man." The *man* will proclaim this man. This will be no painted tyrant, nor will makeup be allowed in the mortal world of true men and women: to Yorick's skull Hamlet says,

Now get you to my lady's chamber, and tell her, let her paint an inch thick, to this favor she must come.

Nor will there be an over-reliance on historionics. "Though I am not splenitive and rash, yet have I in me something dangerous." No more "bloody, bawdy, villain"; we are back to "that within," and it is no longer muddy-mettled. Hamlet patronizingly calls Laertes "a very noble youth"; Hamlet, in learning to act, has grown up.

The play ends with "play," which is swordplay within a dramaturgical context. "Ere I could make a prologue to my brains, they [Rosencrantz and Guildenstern] had begun the play," says Hamlet, referring to the last major movement of Hamlet's action. Hamlet calls the duel spectators "this audience," and "audience to this act," bringing metadramatic implications into a metatheatrical context: *we* are the audience to this act, and to this Act.

Hamlet achieves manhood in death, and heroism through drama. As he lapses into the "rest" which is "silence" and away from the "words, words, words" which have been his undoing, he signals both the end of his life and the end of the play. He completes a metatheatrical odyssey. In the last speech, Fortinbras tells his captains to:

> Bear Hamlet like a soldier to the stage.
> For he was likely, had he been put on
> To have proved most royal.

There are multiple ironies here. Hamlet is cited for his manliness: he is like a soldier (the word comes from *solidus*, meaning solid, particularly as in coinage). But what was it he was to have been "put on?" The phrase dangles provocatively. On a throne, of course to be a king—but if Hamlet were to be put on a stage, as the only available antecedent implies, he would have proven most royal as well. He would not only have made a great king, he would have made a great actor. He would have been one who could play the king, be the king, and, like the player (Richard Burbage) who originally played him, be the king of the players. When, at Irvine, Fortinbras commanded "Go, bid the soldiers shoot," officers fired booming shotgun blasts from the upper corners of the stage. These giant "ejaculations," directly echoing the hunting shotguns fired (at clay pigeons) by Claudius earlier in the Second Act, not only created a thrilling closure for this production of Hamlet, they brought the play to a synthesis of its coming-of-age theme and metatheatrical structure.

No production can "prove" a theory, but the UCI production did at least indicate that the notion of Hamlet's minority is entirely playable and does not befoul the play's dramatic effect. The production ran for two weeks (10 performances) and played to full (450 seat) houses each night. It was also the centerpiece for the 1986 meeting of the University of California Shakespeare Forum, an intercampus association of English and Drama scholars devoted to Shakespearean production; the Forum's symposium brought forward numerous points of view, but no fatal arguments against the play's interpretation, plus considerable praise for the production, the performers, and the highly innovative design.

The primary question raised in advance was whether a young Prince could reflect the profundity of Hamlet's character—and, concurrently, whether a young actor could satisfactorily master the long soliloquies of the part. A tentative answer of *yes* can be posited to both questions. Hamlet's speeches are not, in fact, profoundly mature, and his reflections are not extraordinarily wise—in the sense that Macbeth's or Lear's are. Indeed, they are precisely the sorts of ruminations that are relatively common in a sensitive high school or college student. To be or not to be? What is a man? Am I a coward? These are questions few 16-year-olds manage to avoid. "Why, what an ass am I," is perhaps every adolescent's chief preoccupation. And Paul Lovely, while a relatively inexperienced and untrained actor, and whose voice, like the boy actor's, tended (quite appropriately) to "crack within the ring," proved quite moving in the role, and absolutely masterful at conveying the breathtaking contours of Shakespeare's verse. Indeed, I might suggest that Paul's own consonance with the role itself made his portrayal more effective than any of the three professional actors I saw do the role that same season (at Atlanta, Chicago, and Santa Cruz). Not that Paul was a superior actor but that his juvenility made the scenes with Claudius, the Ghost, and Gertrude (as well as Polonius, Laertes, and Ophelia) far more complex and affecting; and made his bewilderment, inability to control others, and blurred, interwoven states of lucidity and confusion, far more believable. Press reviews tended to confirm that, as did the general reaction of the audience, and (amazingly, since they were mostly more experienced graduate students) the other cast members. That the play held its audience with an attent ear for its four-plus hour length also was evidence that Paul managed to negotiate his way through the part with substantial vividness and dramatic momentum.

The production included several interesting departures. Hamlet's "To be or not to be" was played as a speech to Ophelia, not as a soliloquy. Although this is, as far as I know, something of an innovation, it seems entirely true to the text. Just before Hamlet enters, Polonius tells Ophelia "walk you here," and gives her a book that she is to pretend to read, so that the "show of such an exercise may color your loneliness." Where, on the Globe Theatre stage, could Ophelia have walked, in broad daylight, without Hamlet seeing her? Neither Folio nor Quartos indicate an exit or subsequent re-entrance for Ophelia, and the only justification for playing Hamlet as unaware of her during his speech is when he later calls her "the fair Ophelia" instead of just "fair Ophelia."[11] We simply decided that he spoke to her apostophically, which is less problematical than having Hamlet be blind (on a Shakespearean bare stage!) to her carefully staged "show." Playing the speech to Ophelia makes it a dialogue rather than a soliloquy; not "what shall I do," but "what shall we do?" When Ophelia tacitly rejects the collaboration, and returns the remembrances instead, Hamlet rejects her.

The "Gertrude question" was addressed by having the Queen turn to drink following the closet scene; this gave some justification for Gertrude's vacillating (and/or ambiguous) loyalties following Hamlet's precautions to her, and allowed the actress to play for immediate rather than long-range gratifications: a psychological set that is common in alcoholics. Thus when Claudius hugged her, she let herself enjoy the hug—even though by this point she despised him. The Queen's growing drunkenness provided additional richness to "Gertrude, do not drink!" in the poisoned cup scene.

A pull-down mirror in the set was used to back up certain actions and give them a metatheatrical (audience as spectator) not unlike the Hal Prince production of *Cabaret*. The mirror was revealed for the duels, thus giving them a performative character (as exercises in a mirrored ballet studio), and letting the audience see itself in the process. The mirror appeared one other time in the play—when Hamlet was instructing the Players to "hold the mirror up to nature," and to "show . . . the very age and body of the time his form and pressure." By looking in the mirror, the Players could see the audience: the "nature" and the "age" they were to imitate. But that wasn't all, for, continues Hamlet,

if this [be] overdone or come tardy off, though it make the unskillful
laugh, [it] cannot but make the judicious grieve; the censure of the
which one must in your allowance o'erweigh a whole theatre of others.

Of course, we are the whole theatre of others, and as we look at ourselves in this mirror we must decide if we are the unskillful many or the judicious "one."

NOTES

1 I cannot accept the contextual notions sometimes put forth that there is no delay (since
  Hamlet himself seems to feel there is one) or that there is no occasion for executing

revenge (since Hamlet could easily create one, and rejects the obvious one in the King's closet).

2 When Shakespeare himself was sixteen, his father was taken down to London (Westminister) to defend himself at court against unknown accusations. While the Queen's government could have charged the provincial alderman with remains a mystery, but the teenage Shakespeare must have been terrified of the possible consequences. In 1600, when *Hamlet* was produced, Shakespeare's son, Hamnet, would have been sixteen—however, he had died four years previously. Hamnet, of course, is simply a variant spelling of Hamlet.

3 Actor's emphasis added, of course.

4 The Folio has "rots" which also fulfills this interpretation.

5 "Scullion" is the Folio reading. The Second Quarto reads "stallion," which is usually taken to mean male or female prostitute; in either case less than a man.

6 Shakespeare never titles this play, which Hamlet says "pleased not the million . . . but [had] an honest method," but the quoted speech, he says, is "Aeneas' tale to Dido," and, for convenience in this essay, I am calling the play *Dido and Aeneas*.

7 The duels at UCI—both in the first and last court scenes—were ritualistically prepared. Osric, with a chalk on a long stick, drew a circle on the stage floor while the actors donned a particular kind of cloth helmet with goggles fashionable in German student duelling of the nineteenth century. The precision of the duelling style was memorable, and the audience in the last act immediately recalled the duel of the second scene, which had transpired nearly four hours previously.

8 Attention which has already been paid, of course, in great measure. See, particularly, Maynard Mack's "The World of Hamlet," *Yale Review*, XLI (1952); Howard Felperin's "O'erdoing Termagent," *Yale Review* LXIII (1974); and James Calderwood's *To Be and Not To Be*, Columbia U. Press, 1983.

9 The Players and their playing of *The Murder of Gonzago* serve the plot, of course, by legitimizing the Ghost's tale, but this function is almost entirely gratuitous—plot-sustaining rather than plot-developing—inasmuch as the Ghost's legitimacy needs no confirmation except insofar as Shakespeare wished to throw doubt about it. Shakespeare invented the Players for thematic reasons, and introduced Hamlet's belated suspicion of the Ghost only to prevent the Player scene to seem entirely plot digressive, in my opinion.

10 Most editors assume an omission in the text here, possibly "curb" or "quell."

11 He precedes this with "Soft you now," but this may simply be to stop her from trying to speak at this point, which is how we played it.

CHAPTER

12 Golden Opinions, Sound and Fury

I have bought
Golden opinions from all sorts of people,
Which would be worn now in their newest gloss,
Not cast aside so soon.

Macbeth, to his wife (I.vii.33-34)

One of the unique features of *Macbeth*, Shakespeare's shortest and most concentrated tragedy, is the absence of character development, or even exposition, prior to the onrush of tragic confrontations. King Lear is at relative ease when he ceremoniously divides his kingdom; Othello is in the flush of newly wedded bliss as he addresses the Venetian Senate, and even Hamlet is only sulkily discontented as he taunts the Danish Court. Macbeth, on the other hand, has only a single line about the weather before the Wayward Sisters rekindle his already "fantastical" thought of assassinating Duncan, and Lady Macbeth is in the throes of planning the deed in her first speech. The events of *Macbeth* which ensue are relatively straightforward—there needs to be no book entitled *What Happens in Macbeth*—but there could be a rather fascinating series of speculations on what *doesn't* happen in the play, if only because the lives of the play's two principal characters are, in the play's action, so bound up to their one tragic course of action.

We know, of course, that Macbeth enjoys "golden opinions from all sorts of people" following his great military exploits, and we also know that he finally loses them:

This tyrant, whose sole name blisters our tongues . . .

(Malcolm, IV.iii. 12)

Originally published in *On Stage Studies*, Summer 1987

I grant him bloody,
Luxurious, avaricious, false, deceitful,
Sudden, malicious, smacking of every sin
That has a name . . .

> (Malcolm, IV.iii.57-60)

Those he commands move only in command,
Nothing in love. Now does he feel his title
Hang loose about him, like a giant's robe
Upon a dwarfish thief.

> (Angus, V.ii.20-22)

Macbeth is not unaware of this loss; indeed, he takes full responsibility, knowing at the time of his decision "that we but teach / Bloody instructions, which, being taught, return / To plague th'inventor" (I.vii.8-10). Thus, in the fifth act, Macbeth comments with infinite sadness but no self-pity:

. . . that which should accompany old age,
As honor, love, obedience, troops of friends,
I must not look to have; but in their stead,
Curses not loud but deep . . .

> (V.iii.25-28)

But what about the road not taken? With its golden opinions and newest gloss? What did Macbeth give up? What was the price of his bloody instructions? Granted this may not be a fit subject for strictly literary inquiry ("How many chilblains had Lady Macbeth?"), but it leads to some interesting theatrical possibilities that enrich and concentrate the play by developing its contextual framework. This search, indeed, was a principal task of our 1982 Colorado Shakespeare Festival production.

Productions of *Macbeth* tend to begin in evil and end in horror; this seems to me to falsify the shock of assassination and to trivialize the price of murder. What, after all, is the normal context of assassination? We look back at the recent famous ones: in a theatre in Washington (they were playing a comedy), at a victory celebration in Los Angeles, at a festive military review in Cairo, at ceremonial motorcades in Dallas, the Vatican City, and Sarajevo. Jubilant occasions, most of them, when the guard was down and the spirits up, and the rage of the killers intensified by envy and ill-comparison. And so is the setting for Duncan's murder; at a victory banquet at the home of the celebrated general/thane who brought home first the victory and then the king: at this pleasant-seated castle with its delicate air, ruled by a fair and noble hostess and her full, so valiant lord, wearing, of course, his golden opinions in their newest gloss. Achieving this festive climate on stage last summer argued for setting the play in more recent times—1913 was our decision—to capture the gloss: the sheen of success and the glitter of golden opinions. Medieval burlaps and woolens and furs have tended to bury social distinctions and the sense of occasion in productions of *Macbeth* that are set in the traditional Scots Middle Ages. The road not taken in our production was a road worth looking at: formal dinner parties, champagne soirees, elegant summer banquets, Chinese lanterns, a Palm Court string orchestra, and a glittery, glossy Art Deco setting of silvered steel, black-laquered floors, tuxedoed gentlemen, sequinned ladies, and servants carrying well-laden trays of champagne. A witty urbanity characterized the repartee of the guests: a numbing background for the horror to follow.

Should the setting, the costuming, the lighting, and the acting merely echo and reinforce the action of the play? Or may it serve as a contextual reference point: the basis from which the play's action becomes a departure? "Nothing is but what is not," Macbeth says at the end of his first soliloquy. The action of the play will speak for itself; the setting of the play will speak for "what is not." And the more vividly it speaks, the more sharply Macbeth's choices will be defined.

Macbeth's choices are fully defined in Act I, scene seven, the scene beginning with his soliloquy "If it were done when 'tis done." "We still have judgment here," Macbeth says to himself, as he tries to weigh the rights and wrongs of killing his King, for whom he is kinsman, subject, and host. "We will proceed no further in this business," he concludes, telling his wife about his golden opinions "from all sorts of people." It is a beguiling argument. Creon made it back in Sophocles' *Oedipus Rex* as proof to Oedipus that he, Creon, had no royal ambitions of his own:

CREON: No. Reason it out, as I have done.
Think of this first. Would any sane man prefer
Power, with all a king's anxieties,
To that same power and the grace of sleep?
Certainly not I . . .
As matters stand, I have my way in everything

With your consent, and no responsibilities . . .
 am welcome everywhere; every man salutes me
And those who want your favor seek my ear.
Should I exchange this ease for that anxiety?
> *(Oedipus Rex*, scene two, translated by Dudley Fitts and Robert Fitzgerald)

Creon hangs on to his golden opinions, but then Creon is not a tragic hero—not, at least, in that play. Macbeth's reasoning, and his judgment as well, is turned not by the golden opinions of society, but by the unnervingly precise and penetrating question of his wife:

Art thou afeard?
Wouldst thou . . . live a coward . . . ?
> (I.vii.39-43)

Macbeth asserts his manliness, declaring it consistent with a rational course; she demurs.

MACBETH: I dare do all that may become a man;
Who dares do more is none.
LADY: . . . When you durst do it, then you were a man;
And to be more than what you were, you would
Be so much more the man.
> (I.vii.46-49)

Gender insecurity is a powerful motivating force; Shakespeare has laced the play with it, from Lady Macbeth's unsexing, to her comment that Macbeth is "too full o' th' milk of human kindness," to the ambivalent sexuality of the Wayward Sisters ("You should be women, And yet your beards forbid me to interpret that you are so.") Achieving manhood—in his wife's eyes, not in the world's—is Macbeth's goal, countervailing the golden opinions he is willing to sacrifice in their stead. And so our production sought also to emphasize this "road" as well. Inevitably, the Edwardian elegance of the tuxedoes and champagne gave way to trenchcoated murderers, barebreasted Sisters at the steaming cauldron, owl shrieks in the consuming night, and the relentless beating of drums, blocks, and bells atop the witches' coven.

"I am settled," says Macbeth after his wife's ministrations, and from that time forward his life becomes an hypocrisy: living the champagne life outside, the murderer's inside. "Mock the time with fairest show; / False face must hide what the false heart doth know" (I.vii.81-82). Yes, urges his wife, "Look like th' innocent flower, But be the serpent under't"(I.v.63-64). Hypocrisy has its price, however, which is first seen in excessive drinking, then in madness. In our CSF production, Macbeth drank fairly continuously from his return home: at the party for Duncan (he enters, tie askew, with a champagne glass for his "If it were done" soliloquy); at the time of his first court reception as King, at his scene with the murderers, at his following scene with Lady Macbeth, and, of course, at his banquet for Banquo. "Give me some wine!" he shakily orders (in this production) after Banquo's ghost has first disappeared. The servant pours wine into his glass. About to drink, Macbeth notices the glass is but half full. "Fill full!" he shouts violently. The servant drops his tray; trembling, he fills Macbeth's glass. The guests are stunned, appalled. Macbeth smiles crazily at his dumbrounded subjects. "I drink to the general joy o' th' whole table, / And to our dear friend Banquo . . . To all, and him, we thirst." He tosses down his drink, awaits a refill. This is alcoholism with a Royal We.

Macbeth is not the only character to drink in the play, of course. Lady Macbeth has used her wine and wassail not only to drug the grooms but to embolden herself to her deed. The Porter makes clear that drinking "provokes the desire." And Macbeth's guests share in the drinking feast prepared in Banquo's absence. The ambivalence of a drinker's pleasure (it is "an equivocator" says the Porter) is nowhere more clear than in Lady Macbeth's plaint to her husband when he fails to give the banquet toast: "My royal lord, You do not give the cheer" (III.iv.32-33). Never has drinking been less cheery than here.

Drinking gives way to insanity midway through the play; a mental derangement caused by sleeplessness (cf. Creon), guilt, and the after-effects of alcohol itself. "O full of scorpions is my mind, O wife!" cries Macbeth. And she, "a mind diseased," at the end of the play, begging her husband to bed (for sleep? for sex?) in a sleepwalking reverie. It didn't work out. Not only have they lost the golden opinions, they have lost each other. "Are you a man?" demands Lady Macbeth when Macbeth flees from the banquet at the sight of Banquo's ghost. "Strange things I have in head," he says at the end of the scene. Whatever they are, they don't include her. "Come on," she says, "sleek o'er your rugged looks." But the sleekness, the gloss, is gone forever. "Make our faces vizards to our hearts," Macbeth replies. Let's become actors and put on masks.

Macbeth is not a moral man, but he wrestles long and hard with moral questions; indeed, he's the only person in the play who does. Yet he certainly comes up with wrong answers. Part of his problem is a preoccupation with outward forms, including those golden opinions "which would be worn." Worn? When Cassio, in *Othello*, laments the loss of his reputation, it is clearly something he thinks of as *inside* himself, not just a garment:

IAGO: . . . are you hurt? . . .
CASSIO: Ay, past all surgery . . .Reputation, reputation; reputation! O, I have lost my reputation! I have lost the immortal part of myself . . .
(II.iii.59-64)

Cassio's reputation is spiritual, beyond surgery, much less mere tailoring. But Macbeth's honors have "come to him Like our strange garments," and—so he seems to think—are easily exchanged for something better on the rack. The preoccupation with externals and appearances, with opinions that are worn, false faces that hide, and vizards that mask, are the preoccupation of an actor, not a general nor a king, nor even, perhaps, of a healthy individual.

Shakespeare draws a rather precise antonymic parallel between Macbeth and King Lear in the opposition of inner health and outer garment:

LEAR: . . . Take physic, pomp;
Expose thyself to feel what wretches feel,
That thou may shake the superflux to them . . .
Off, off, you lendings! Come, unbutton here . . .
(III.iii.33-35, 110)

MACBETH: Throw physic to the dogs! I'll none of it!
Come, put mine armor on!
(V.iii.47-48)

Both lines are followed by frustrated attempts at recostuming; Lear starts stripping, but is stopped by the fool; Macbeth tries to arm himself, but even with Seyton's assistance he can't seem to manage the buckle. Crucial to both scenes is the acceptance or rejection of "physic," or psychotherapy: Lear takes it, Macbeth spurns it, rejecting the Doctor and his doctoring, and putting on his armor instead. He will die "with harness on my back"; no shaking of the superflux for this Scots warrior.

Dressing oneself for the role is, of course, the task of the actor; in taking that course, rather than in stripping down to the "bare forked animal" essentials of *King Lear*, Macbeth seeks to recover the golden opinions in a theatricalized form. If he can no longer have the love of the thanes, he can have the admiration of the audience. If he can no longer be a great general/king, he can be a great tragic hero. Macbeth finally abandons the road not taken: he abandons it in his mind as well as in reality. He abandons the cheap hypocrisy and false facing of his early "acting" adventures, and takes on the burden of a tragic persona reckless with insistence on meeting his fate:

Strange things I have in head, that will to hand,
Which must be acted ere they may be scanned.
(III.iv.139-140)

Acted in what sense? Done, of course, but also playacted: playacted before analyzed for scansion. Macbeth had earlier urged that his "eye wink at the hand," but now he is giving his hand—his acting—free reign. "From this moment, / The very firstlings of my heart shall be / The firstlings of my hand" (IV.i.148-149). He will play the role to the hilt. Thus the transition of Macbeth from agonized social climber/moral-wrestler to Macbeth the reckless actor-playactor, strutting and fretting his hour upon the stage, hollering defiantly at the elements ("Blow, wind, come wrack!") and trying his last with swashbuckling aplomb. "Lay on, Macduff, / And damned be him that first cries, hold, enough" (V.viii.33-34). Were *Macbeth* not a tragedy of playacting, that line could only be sheer melodrama.

"My name's Macbeth," Macbeth trumpets to young Siward at the end of the play. "The devil himself could not pronounce a title / More hateful to mine ear," responds the young soldier (V.vi.9-11). Title? Of a play, perhaps. A play called *Macbeth*. A play about a man who did something very wrong, who knew it was wrong yet had good reasons—so he thought—to do it anyway, and who eventually lost a great deal of sleep over the whole thing. A man who was shallow enough to think that morality was something that could be worn, evil enough to refuse his medicine when it became inevitable, profound enough to come to grips with the sheer totality of his actions, and existential enough to make the most of them through the intensity of his commitment. At this point the character of Macbeth and the play of *Macbeth* come together. At midpoint: "cabined, cribbed, confined, bound in." At the end: "Before my body I throw my warlike shield." No Button Moulder for him. No golden opinions either.

But rather the sublimity of a tragic existence at the edge of the absolute; a superlative performance in the face of a tale told by an idiot, a lively and sensing being at one with his black and deep desires, plunging into the sound and fury with his eyes wide open.

CHAPTER

13 Quince's Moon: Disfiguring Reality in *A Midsummer Night's Dream*

A Midsummer Night's Dream concludes with the unfailingly comic play-within-a-play, *The Most Lamentable Comedy, and Most Cruel Death, of Pyramus and Thisbe.* This is a backstage gag, of course: a group of amateurs doing a wretched job with a serious play, and *Pyramus* has become quite independently famous: it's often performed as a one-act play all by itself. But *Pyramus* is absolutely crucial to its parent play, *Dream*, although this is infrequently recognized.

Dream is a play about—among other things—putting on a play (and why); during the course of *Dream* we see *Pyramus* selected, cast, rehearsed, performed, and evaluated. And, because *Pyramus* is written and performed by amateurs who, quite possibly, have never even seen a play, we see how they have to first invent a concept of theatre and a notion of theatricality; these Athenians, like Aeschylus and Aristophanes before them, have to create an entire dramaturgy in order to put on their play. I think some of Shakespeare's deepest ideas of theatre art come into these sequences.

In Act III, Peter Quince discovers that, inasmuch as his characters of Pyramus and Thisbe are to meet by moonlight, his theatre company must "bring moonlight into the chamber" where the play is performed. How can he do this? He poses the problem to his company. It is first suggested that the moon may actually shine that night—so an almanac is found, and the performers-to-be discover that, yes, the moon does indeed shine on the night of the performance. Good, exults Bottom, "then may you leave a casement of the great window, where we play, open, and the moon may shine in."

"No," says Peter Quince, after some reflection, rather "One must come in with a bush of thorns and a lantern, and say he comes to disfigure or to present the person of Moonshine."

Originally published in *On Stage Studies*, Summer 1989

Why "disfigure?" Why isn't the real moon sufficient? And why did Shakespeare take such pains to establish the fact that the moon indeed shone—just so that Quince could reject it?

The reason is, of course, that reality isn't a play; and it's a play, not reality, that Quince has been commissioned to produce. What is the difference between reality and play? Simply that a play is *meaningful,* while reality is not.

A play is composed of signs and indications. Add them up and you get something: meaning, perhaps, or a resolution of conflicting (and identified) issues, or at least identification itself. Life, on the other hand, is a "poor player"; as Macbeth discovers, it is "full of sound and fury, signifying nothing." Life has no indications: it is mere random phenomena.

This is the fundamental principle of semiotics: the sometime science of significations. Art, with its (consciously or unconsciously) contrived signifiers, indicates a multiplicity of definable and perceivable categories, alignments, structures, and directions. The ingredients of a play (or any work of art) "disfigure" (to use Quince's word) reality in order to present (and impersonate) it "significantly" (the semiotician's word), or indicatively, or meaningfully. Significations can be summed, subtracted, targeted, adopted, countered. The material moon is merely an unsignifying and therefore fundamentally "insignificant" phenomenon of natural reality; in order to create a significant (or meaningful) moon, a dramatic integer (here, a character) must come in to "disfigure" or to "present the idea of" moon. Drama is necessarily abstract, Quince reasons, because drama's raw material is ideas.

Bottom gets the point. "Some man or other must present Wall," he declares. A wall cannot present a wall, because a wall simply is a wall. A wall would be mistaken for a wall, and would therefore not indicate a wall. Wallness, too, must be meaningful, not phenomenal.

The presenter of Wall says:

In this same interlude it doth befall
That I one Snout by name present a Wall.

Watching *Pyramus,* the *Dream* audience makes good sport of the laughable contradictions between the real actor and the signifying character: Snout is a "witty partition," a "sensible (meaning sensate) wall," a "rased mural," and a "willful wall." Snout is enraged at being made mock of, but, being a Wall, he cannot respond. He is trapped in his signifying mode. The *Dream* audience makes even more fun of Moonshine when he comes in:

> *Starveling:* This lantern doth the horned moon present.
> Myself, the man in the moon do seem to be.

Starveling, overwhelmed by ontological panic, has abandoned his directed disfigurement. Since the Act Three rehearsal, Starveling has decided that, as a man, he cannot satisfactorily present moonshine in his own person; but he can perhaps "seem to be" the man in the moon, which (he figures) is man-like enough to bear scrutiny. He will let the lantern present the horned moon.

It doesn't work: the *Dream* audience won't buy it. Starveling's lantern is not a crescent for one thing, and if Starveling's person were to be the "man" in the moon, he would have to be in his lantern, not holding it. And the dog and bush would have to be in the lantern too. Starveling mistakenly relies on reality, not dramaturgy. In trying to be literal, he becomes semiotically diffuse. He becomes, as Gogo says in *Godot*, "really insignificant."

Shakespeare's point is that literal reality is not the best guide for shaping a meaningful acting performance; literal reality (the sound and fury) only diffuses meaning and confounds signification.

Pyramus and Thisbe goes on to its cathartic coda, and, of course, it's all utterly hilarious. A mixed doggerel verse, home-made props, home-made animals, Thisbe's drag costume and make-up, and universal ham directing and acting: we, like the *Dream* audience, become a dream audience.

But *Pyramus* becomes oddly moving, too. "Beshrew my heart, but I pity the man," says the Duchess, meaning the man Pyramus, not the man Bottom. *Pyramus* is a fiction in which *Dream* audience and dream audience are induced to believe—with amusement as incentive and reward. By play's end, the Duke's party (and Shakespeare's audience) should all be moved. In Colorado, Thisbe (played by Flute in drag, with a "beard coming") called Hippolyta, Hermia, and Helena to his side as the "lovers" to "make moan" at Pyramus' death—the three lovers were now Flute/Thisbe's (for here the play-actor and play-character were joined) Three Sisters:

> O Sisters Three,
> Come, come to me

and they came, awkwardly but determinedly, to share in their universal lament of socially compromised and/or corrupted love. *Pyramus* characters and *Dream* characters conjoined with each other, and with a summer Colorado audience; playacting and playgoing together on the theme of love on trial.

In part, we are moved by this ridiculous scene precisely as Theseus has predicted:

Love, therefore, and tongue-tied simplicity
At least speak most . . .

The rank amateurs' devotion to their roles, their love for each other and of the theatre, and their truly tongue-tied simplicity (forgotten lines, forgotten roars, awkwardness, and panic) has spoken most, and wins our amused affection.

But in greater measure, the mechanicals' disfiguring of reality has framed and transformed the reality of the lovers. It has overtaken the wry wittiness of the court—which is a disfiguring of another (and cheaper) sort, and replaced it with a meaningful structure, a shape worthy of a fairy blessing. For *Pyramus* is intended, as Theseus says:

To wear away this long age of three hours
Between our after-supper and bed-time . . .

One would think that these newly married couples could go to their bed-time whenever they wanted. In the forest, certainly, copulation thrived. Until now, *Dream* has been what we must consider an erotic play, even if the penetrations have been limited to the divinely bestial (Titania and Bottom/Ass) and playfully linguistic—with wordplaying "disfigures of speech" (the verbal technician can identify anaphora, isocolon, epizeuxis, parison, epistrophe, antimetabole, anadiplosis, ploce, epanolepsis, polyptoton, paronomasia, and antanaclasis) such as can be found in greater quantity than anywhere else in the Shakespearean canon. But Theseus asks:

Is there no play
To ease the anguish of a torturing hour?

These hours—those between the wedding banquet and the wedding night—are now "torturing," and Theseus and the lovers, three on three, require "play" before they go to bed.

It is in *Pyramus* that word play and sex play come together, in significant play: under Quince's disfigured moon.

So the rude mechanicals "disfigure" reality by putting on their play: they semioticize it, making love and sex (archaic passions) into a comprehensible, organized (and therefore meaningful) set of significant, if often amusing, associations. The only reality, Shakespeare might have forecast, is perceived reality (artfully) contrived; the rest is mere phenomenal chaos.

CHAPTER

14 Oedipus and the Absurd Life

The theatre is a living medium, and one of the aspects of the greatness of *Oedipus Tyrannus* is that it can be produced with modern actors before a modern audience with stunning dramatic results. The lapse of 2,500 years has done nothing to still the anguish of Oedipus's quest, nor the magnificence of his defeat. Quite simply, *Oedipus Tyrannus* is a play which receives its force from an uncompromised, penetrating analysis of the human predicament; a play which will excite empathic response as long as our race endures.

The "stuff" of Oedipus is human identity. It must be clear by now that this is not a play about the evils of murdering strangers at crossroads, but a demonstration of a man slamming into his own self at an inopportune and unguarded moment. It is a wholly archetypal play, set in a primitive, precivilized environment and unappeased by subplots, comedic refreshments, romance, or discursive choral reflections. Its strength is in its directness and purity; also its inevitability. As French playwright Jean Giraudoux once remarked, *"Le plus bête des hommes voit toujours assez clair pour devenir aveugle."* Even the stupidest man will always see clearly enough to blind himself.

Oedipus is a *tyrannus*. The word cannot now be fairly translated, but it certainly does not mean "king." It is important to remember that *Oedipus* is *not* set in the sophisticated, brilliant, arty world of Sophocles. The story was sung by Homer three centuries previous to its fifth century dramatization, and was a distant legend even in Homer's time; part of the Aegean mythic history which predates Christ by more than a millennium. In reaching back into prehistory, Sophocles found an unstructured political-ethical cosmos which allowed free reign to the primitive forces he lets loose. Shakespeare did much the same in *Macbeth* and *King Lear*. Oedipus is not a "king," with all the modern legal implications of primogeniture and constitutionalism. He is simply a tribal chief; or the lead wolf in the wolfpack, who receives his position

Originally published in the Norton Critical Edition of the *Oedipus Tyrannus*, 1969 through brute power and loses it the moment he can no longer exert that power. When in the course of the play Oedipus is defeated and Creon takes his place, the chorus simply watches and attests to the changeover; there is neither formal abdication nor legal re-investiture. It is like the old wolf cowering blindly into exile while the others growl and turn their obeisance to the next in line.

As a *tyrannus* Oedipus does not overly excite our admiration. His characterization is rather flat; he is a man in a state of appalling ignorance, who lives in dread that the sky is about to fall on him and that he will be unable to do anything about it. He is a strong man, presumably (he did manage the murder at the crossroads), but not unusually bright. His ability to decipher the riddle of the Sphinx has been much misinterpreted. Riddles are for children, particularly that one, and Oedipus's ability to solve it indicates no genius; simply an uncluttered, and fairly imaginative mind. "Then I came—ignorant Oedipus— came and smothered her," he brags to Teiresias. He is stubborn, bullheaded, frequently stupid, often rude, and admittedly and unashamedly untutored; in short, a primitive, pre-Hellenic chieftain.

Oedipus believes he is questing truth in the search for the murderer of Laius, as ordered by the oracle at Delphi. But in actuality he is following Delphi's more general imperative: "Know thyself!" There are actually two Oedipus's in the play. There is the foundling, son of Laius and Jocasta, who has his feet pierced and is left to die on Cithaeron. And there is the tyrant, son of Polybus and Merope, who destroys the Sphinx and becomes tyrannus of Thebes and husband of Jocasta. In a metaphoric sense, these are Oedipus's inner (the foundling) and outer (the tyrant) identities. They remain separate for a generation, yet they come crashing together at the play's climax, and the collision is like nuclear fusion. The synthesis of identities, a monstrous adhesion, creates a new Oedipus, one ready as neither before him to go to Colonus; one crippled by the discovery of the human predicament and yet ennobled by reaching a harmony of identities. Oedipus, at the conclusion of the play and after a terrible agony, knows himself.

It is important to stress the routine nature of this conflict. All men suffer a dual identity: the one that they inwardly feel and the one they receive from the outer world. One man to himself is a generous and Christian patriot; to his neighbors he is a bigot. Another to himself is a morally corrupt failure; yet to his colleagues he is a great scientist. Goethe's great Faust capitulates to the difference between his self-opinion and the opinions of those around him. Virtually all men suffer from their inability to unite their failures with their ambitions, and their successes with their self-doubts. *Oedipus Tyrannus* merely characterizes this divorce, this confrontation with oneself.

It goes without saying that most men end up in some sort of adjustment with themselves, or at least find a means to reconcile this confrontation. Most live within the forced dialectic between their conflicting identities, and maintain for themselves an uneasy alliance, perhaps sadly but equably. Some drown the confrontation in alcohol, some give in to it consciously (suicide) or unconsciously (schizophrenia), and some join in an alliance with it and live on what Sartre calls "the far side of despair." Most often these are peaceable and undramatic responses to the accepted human condition. Oedipus, since his moment of self-realization comes upon him so suddenly and with such gruesome details, is a figure for grand tragedy. He finds that Oedipus the tyrant has feet of clay—literally the pierced and swollen feet which gave him his name—and that in fact he is Oedipus the foundling, the parricide, the mother-lover. The moment is catastrophic. It is the fundamental question of man of any age—"Who am I?"—pursued resolutely and dogmatically to its shattering end. Whereas a wiser, better-adjusted man would simply let the dialectic ride and the questions go unanswered, Oedipus perseveres. This—his terrible persistence—determines his heroic character.

Oedipus's case is an extreme one, which makes *Oedipus Tyrannus* more than simply a credible narrative. His crime was enormous, grotesque. Even without Freud's landmark discoveries about mother-incest, we can appreciate that this was one of the most egregious sins of antiquity; had it not been, Sophocles would no doubt have chosen a different story. And Oedipus's reaction is fully commensurate to his deed. He tears out his eyes, a total repudiation of his willingness to seek truth and to merge his two warring identities. If there could ever be a moral to this play it would be this: that to find yourself is at the same time to destroy yourself.

Oedipus is a ritualized mimetic drama; a classic example of the play which is, in Aristotle's words, the imitation of an action. Structurally, it is one of the simplest plays ever written; Oedipus seeks the truth, finds it, and acts upon it. There is precious little discussion or sidetracking; and there is no thematic opposition to the main line of the play. To succeed in such a simple work, Sophocles had to create it in a scale of majestic proportions, and he did. *Oedipus* is a vertical play of towering magnitude, of great sustained power and cruelty. The action gathers force and snowballs to an inexorable conclusion, picking up speed with geometric progression, moving from pole to pole in little more than an hour. The dialogue is spare and direct, filled with questions and cross-examinations, void of reflections and rhetorical indulgences. The chorus echoes the tragedy more than it engages in it, and it thereby heightens the play's tone of incantation. *Oedipus* begins with a ceremony of lamentation and ends with the symbolic *sparagmos,* or tearing asunder of the hero, as was done to Dionysus in the ancient dithyrambs, and to Osiris in the Egyptian Passion Plays. *Oedipus* is a religious, not an intellectual drama. It is religious despite the fact that nothing in the play presumes a deistic philosophy. It is a celebration rather than an analysis of man's search for himself; a ritualization of his internal confrontation. Sophocles, having discovered the essential human duality, seeks not to explain or solve it, but merely to expose it mercilessly in a terrible rite of expiation. This ritualization of man's intrinsic anguish is the basic ingredient of the contemporary genre: the theatre of the absurd.

Most theories of tragedy insist that tragedy must be ennobling. Presumably, this is a refinement of the well-known Aristotelian concept that tragedy "purges" our pity and terror through some emotional upheaval. Tragedy, we are thereupon led to believe, enlightens us to the superior order and harmony of the cosmos. Such theories are often advanced to explain and justify the dismal fate of Oedipus which Sophocles stages for us, but we must be forgiven if we find them unacceptable. *Oedipus* concludes in an overt affirmation of man's failure and his despair. When Jocasta has destroyed herself, and Oedipus, his eye sockets gored and bloody, returns to the stage, the chorus (and audience) are profoundly shaken. Pathetically, Oedipus begs for his daughters (denied) and for some directions (also denied). Creon, aghast at the events which have led to his assumption of power, gropes for policy; we know that his reign will hardly be less wretched. As Oedipus stumbles away and Creon unsteadily attempts to salvage the city, the chorus—who after all this cannot find a single reason to explain what has happened to them—merely reminds itself and us that "none of us mortals / can truly be thought of as happy / until he is granted deliverance from life / until he is dead / and must suffer no more." Man's feebleness, ruthlessly demonstrated, is crushingly and unambiguously confirmed.

What *Oedipus* gives us, positively, is not a purgation of this despair, but an enthusiasm for Oedipus's single great quality: his absurd courage. This becomes the motive force of the play. Oedipus, as he begins to see where he is going, secretly delights in it. He assumes his identity with absurd conviction. Labeled a bastard in Corinth, he rushes to Delphi to investigate. Labeled a parricide by Teiresias, he propels his questions to everyone in sight. "I have to hear!" he shouts to the panic-stricken Shepherd. Though he sees himself sinking into a vortex, he plunges deeper and faster on his own accord. Galvanized by the inevitable, he charges into the chaos of his own existence, and bears his own responsibility. He refuses to blame the gods: "It was Apollo. He brought this pain, this suffering to me. *But it was my hand that struck the blow!*" he cries. Oedipus is a man in absurd revolt against his duality. He defies the oracles at the same time he is submitting to them. He refuses to turn back his search, he refuses to accept Jocasta's proffered compromise, he refuses to alter his collision course with destiny. He becomes an absurd hero.

In *The Myth of Sisyphus,* Camus defines the absurd life as a "permanent revolution," and defines revolt as "a constant confrontation between man and his own obscurity." These concepts are, I think, applicable here; perhaps more applicable than Aristotle's pronouncements of catharsis and peripeteia. Oedipus's ennobling quality is his commitment to the impossible, his quest into the darkness of human existence. He follows this quest to its final depth—and finds himself. This is Sophocles' most shattering irony: Oedipus confronts obscurity and finds Oedipus. Oedipus foundling and Oedipus *tyrannus* are one. He has accepted the absurd, challenged it, and borne the responsibility of losing to it. Blind, proud, and with a profounder power, Oedipus stumbles on to Colonus, like Beckett's Pozzo on the way to Saint Saviour, held up by his awesome dignity. Creon is left to his own blindness.

CHAPTER

15 Weil's God and Beckett's Godot

*This essay was written in 1959, when there wasn't yet a single book written on the
work of Samuel Beckett; today, a computerized search of the University of California
library system yields over 700 individual volumes sporting his name. Yet the essay's central
argument, although its methodology is clearly of its time, bears a current hearing, particularly
considering the continuing scholarly and popular interest in the work of Simone Weil.*

✦ ✦ ✦

Waiting for Godot is one of the most controversial plays to be widely published and
produced in the post-war era, for beyond its extraordinary theatrical values and unique
humor lies an apparent pattern of symbolism which has fluttered the imagination of
audiences and critics unceasingly. Most often given and debated among the many
"interpretations" of the play are those modeled along the lines of Christian theology.
In February 1956, the *London Times Literary Supplement* published an article inter-
preting the play "more or less as a Christian parable."[1] In discussing the results of that
article the paper said, "The article evoked a long and excited correspondence in which
Mr. Beckett's play was claimed in turn by Christians, atheistic existentialists, nihilists,
and Nietzscheans."[2] Recently one of the nihilists has said of Beckett, "his pessimism is
deeper than any ever expressed; there is no evidence whatever of compassion or of a
Christian approach."[3] This essay postulates a Christian interpretation based specifically on a comparison of Beckett's play and works with the religious essays of the French
theologian, Simone Weil.

Weil was born in Paris in 1909, making her three years younger than Beckett, an
Irishman. They both came to the famed *Ecole Normale Superior* in 1928, Beckett as

Originally published in *Modern Drama*, Summer 1964

Lecteur d'Anglais and Weil as a student of philosophy. At that time the school was a burning intellectual center; also studying there was Jean Paul Sartre. In 1930 and 1932 Beckett and Weil left the *Ecole* and lived during the most part of the next twelve years in Paris and southern France, and although their acquaintance has never been authenticated, it may be presumed. Simone Weil became quickly recognized by her intellectual confrères; André Gide called her "the most truly spiritual writer of this century."[4] Beckett spent the '30s in companionship with James Joyce, publishing short stories, poems, and a novel before going into hiding in the Vaucluse country during the war. After the liberation, he wrote his best known works including his plays and the trilogy of novels entitled *The Namable—Molloy, Malone Dies,* and *The Unnamable.* His play in question, *Waiting For Godot,* was published in 1952, one year after the posthumous publication of Weil's selected essays, entitled *Waiting For God.*

Weil's major concern in this work is with a set of characters she calls "the afflicted," characters not unlike the strange persons who inhabit the Beckett landscape. In one essay, "The Love of God and Affliction," she states,

> Affliction is something inseparable with physical suffering and yet quite distinct
> . . . made irresistibly present to the soul by the attack or immediate apprehension
> of physical pain . . . The event that has seized and uprooted a life attacks it,
> directly or indirectly, in all its parts, social, psychological, and physical. As for
> those who have been struck by one of these blows that leaves a being struggling
> on the ground like a half-crushed worm, they have no words to express what is
> happening to them. Every innocent being in his affliction feels himself accursed.
> Men struck down by affliction are at the foot of the Cross, almost at the greatest
> possible distance from God. Affliction is anonymous before all things; it deprives
> its victims of their personality and makes them into things.

Beckett has created in his works of fiction at the level of Weil's world of imagery; his poetic analysis resembles the sketched details of Weil's afflicted and their universe, and his characters seem to personify the worm-like afflicted of her imagination. The most extraordinary example of this character is the multiple hero Moran-Molloy-Malone-Macmann-Worm in *The Namable* who says of himself at the end of a life-long journey towards total deterioration and affliction, "Worm, to say that he does not know who he is, what is happening, is to underestimate him." Worm is the extreme example of affliction, as he is totally bereft of sensory experience, personality, and humanity. In the relative clarity of the Cackon country (the setting for *Godot)* however, Beckett explores more varied degrees of affliction.

The two principal characters, Vladimir and Estragon, have lost their identity before the play begins. They call themselves by the pet names of Gogo and Didi, yet are addressed or address themselves as Mr. Albert, Adam, and Catulle (in the French version). In their anonymity they are lost to society, and when Vladimir laments, "nobody ever recognizes us," his words are proven true. (Weil: Affliction is anonymous.") Their attitude is the defeatism of the worm, expressed in worm-like images in Estragon's truisms, "No use struggling . . . no use wriggling." (Weil: "struggling on the ground like a half-crushed worm.") The physical pain of affliction is with them always, made "irresistibly present" by Vladimir's kidney ailment and Estragon's aching feet and continual beatings, whether real or imagined. Their pathetic plight is summed up by their own cries, "I don't know what to think anymore." (Weil: "they have no words to express what is happening to them"), and "I'm accursed." (Weil: "Every innocent being in his affliction feels himself accursed.")

Pozzo and Lucky, who visit the two men in the two acts (supposedly successive days) of the play show a marked progression into affliction between the acts. Pozzo in the first act mildly suffers under the duress of human existence, exhibiting pride in ownership and in his own marvellous identity. By the end of that act, however, he is already shaken by his knowledge of his failing powers and by the loss of his possessions (pulverizer, pipe, and pocket watch), and at his second entrance he exhibits attacks "social, psychological, and physical" by being blinded, in great physical pain, and totally unsocial. His progression into affliction is duplicated by Lucky who had not so far to go; a totally possessed slave in the first act, Lucky loses his sole remaining contact with the world, speech, in the second act and only responds to "a taste of (the) boot, in the face and the privates as far as possible." His having a name at all is a joke, like a frontiersman naming his rifle, and he has become completely a thing without human values. "Affliction," says Weil, "deprives its victims of their personality and makes them into things." Certainly Beckett's characters check in with all of the qualifications for membership in Weil's afflicted.

Weil's people are, as the title of her book suggests, waiting for God, while Beckett's hapless souls are waiting (at least apparently) for someone else. But over the denial of Beckett himself ("If I knew what Godot was I would have said so,")[5] the reasons for linking Godot with the deity are plentiful and obvious, and stand corroborated by the personal evidence of Beckett himself. The most direct examination of the play reveals that Godot stands for salvation of one form or another:

VLADIMIR: We'll hang ourselves tomorrow. Unless Godot comes.
ESTRAGON: And if he comes?
VLADIMIR: We'll be saved.

VLADIMIR: It's Godot! At last! Gogo! It's Godot! We're saved!

A distinct link is provided by Lucky's one speech and a statement by the boy:

LUCKY: Given the existence of a personal God . . . with white beard . . .

VLADIMIR: Has he a beard, Mr. Godot?
BOY:Yes Sir.
VLADIMIR: Fair or . . . (he hesitates) . . . or black?
BOY: I think it's white Sir.
VLADIMIR: Christ have mercy on us.

One passage contains three specific allusions which indicate that Godot is Christ, referring to the Bible, to Beckett's early works, and to the French version of this play in contrast to the English (both of course written by Beckett). The passage is in Act One, and follows "a fright":

VLADIMIR: I thought it was he.
ESTRAGON: Who?
VLADIMIR: Godot.
ESTRAGON:.Pah. The wind in the reeds.
VLADIMIR: I could have sworn I heard shouts.
ESTRAGON: And why would he shout?
VLADIMIR: At his horse.
ESTRAGON: (in French version) *Allons-nous-en.*
VLADIMIR: (in French version) *Ou? Ce soir on couchera peut-être chez lui, au chaud, au sec . . .*

The wind in the reeds alludes to the book of Matthew where Jesus confronts the multitudes who were vainly seeking John the Baptist. Jesus said unto them, "What went ye out in the wilderness to see? A reed shaken by the wind?" Jesus berates them for seeking a false prophet; Christ, and in this case Godot, are the real and unlocated prophets. The second item is that of Christ on horseback, which is a familiar Beckett image. In *All That Fall* Mrs. Rooney contemplates at length on the horse, or hinny, and her problem sends her to a theology student from whom she gets the answer, "Yes, it was a hinny, he rode into Jerusalem or wherever it was on a hinny. (pause) That must mean something," and in *Embers* Henry cries for "Christ! Hooves! Hooves! Christ!"[6] The third allusion is wholly internal; by attributing to Godot's house the qualities of warmth *(chaud)* and dryness *(sec)* Beckett refers to a later line in which these same qualities are attributed to Christ's residence,

> VLADIMIR: You're not going to compare yourself with Christ . . . where he lived it was warm, it was dry.

In a private correspondence, Beckett has implied the consciousness of the allusion by admitting that the omission of the "*au chaud, au sec*" line was a "mistake and should be restored."[7]

If we can then assume, even conditionally, that Beckett's Godot is or is like God, and that his characters are or are like Weil's afflicted, the presentation of the basic situation in Weil and in Beckett throws each into clearer focus when seen in the light of the other. Their title theme is *waiting,* with the emphasis on the *passive* reception of salvation. Weil says point-blankly: "We are incapable of progressing vertically. God crosses the universe and comes to us. He comes at his own time. We have the power to consent to receive him or to refuse." This system is brutally fatalistic, and it is expressed in the very first line of Beckett's play, to be repeated again and again, "Nothing to be done." Vladimir and Estragon realize from the start their hopeless position, that they must, in Estragon's words, "Simply wait." "Hand in hand from the top of the Eiffel tower. . . . Now it's too late. They wouldn't even let us up," comments Vladimir, incapable of progressing vertically, and Estragon comes to the more general conclusion: "Don't let's do anything, it's safer." But in awaiting Godot they do have the single choice left of whether or not to accept his offerings: "I'm curious to see what he has to offer," says Vladimir, "Then we'll take it or leave it."

The futility of action described by Beckett and Weil is paralleled by the equal impossibility of intellectual examination. Weil says: "There is a special way of waiting upon truth . . . yet not allowing ourselves to go out in search of it." Beckett describes the situation comically through Vladimir, "When you seek, you hear . . . that prevents you from finding . . . that prevents you from thinking." We can attest to the seriousness of Beckett's expression here by finding the same thought in *Watt* published ten years previously, where Watt realizes that "When you cease to think you start to find."

The situation (waiting) is in both writers pinned to a specific topography. *Waiting for Godot* takes place alongside a road which we are told (in the French version) leads to "St. Saviour." The only stage elements are a mound and a tree. If we are not thereby reminded of Calvary and Cross (and we should be), the author presses home this comparison by beginning the play's argument with a worried questioning of the four gospel accounts of the Crucifixion, and particularly the two thieves that were executed beside Christ. He then allows that the tree has the power of resurrection, for when Estragon suggests hanging himself from it Vladimir protests, "You'd get an erection . . . with all that follows. Where it falls the mandrakes grow, that's why they shriek when you pull them up." Beckett has used the mandrake as a symbol of this kind of resurrection (into greater affliction) before. In *Molloy*, Moran describes to his son a fall he took which signaled his metamorphosis into the more afflicted Molloy. Describing that significant event, Moran said, " 'A fall . . . did you never have a fall.' I tried to remember the name of the plant that springs from the ejaculations of the hanged and shrieks when plucked." This is of course the mandrake again. That Moran is resurrected into Molloy has been noticed by many critics[8] and follows the established Beckett pattern in which characters move, usually by their own volition, into a state of more complete affliction—as the hero of *Murphy* who wanted to become one of the hapless insane for whom he cared.

Weil, as Beckett, sets her action on the exact site of the Crucifixion. "Men struck down by affliction are at the foot of the Cross," she claims, adding that this is "almost at the greatest possible distance from God." That the Cross is so greatly removed from God is central to Weil's thought, which at this point becomes particularly unique. Holding that the only possibility of perfection for us on earth is extreme affliction (which implies the almost perfect absence of God rather than the impossible, flesh-prevented presence of Him), then at this greatest distance between God and man, God is paradoxically more accessible. The bridging of this great distance was symbolized, in Weil's terms, by the Crucifixion in which Christ felt himself abandoned and accursed, and yet loved God wholly. Over this distance, Weil says,

God crosses the universe and comes to us. We have the power to consent to receive him or to refuse . . . If we consent, God puts a little seed in us and he goes away again. From that moment God has no more to do; neither have we, except to wait. When the seed of divine love placed in us has grown and become a tree [we must] . . . take it back to its origin. We know quite well in what likeness this tree is made . . . [*i.e.*, the Cross] . . . It was the seed of this tree that God placed within us. . . . It is this tree which has grown within us and has become ineradicable.

This process is exactly the one to which Vladimir and Estragon submit themselves. At the very beginning of the play Vladimir tries (and fails) to remember the proverb: "Hope deferred maketh the heart sick, but when desire cometh it is a tree of life."[9] After Moran's "resurrection," previously referred to in the novel *Molloy*, Moran muses, in regard to his umbrella, "I found that when I leaned upon it the heaviness in my leg . . . disappeared even more quickly than when I stood supported only by my muscles and the tree of life." In the same way Vladimir is waiting for desire to be fulfilled, for Godot to come, and for the tree of life to grow within him. And there is in the play one test made to see if the tree has already grown. In the first act, the two men "do the tree."

> VLADIMIR: Let's do the tree, for the balance.
> ESTRAGON: The tree? (Vladimir does the tree, staggering about on one leg.)
> VLADIMIR: (stopping). Your turn. (Estragon does the tree, staggers.)
> ESTRAGON: Do you think God sees me?
> VLADIMIR: You must close your eyes.
> ESTRAGON: (Estragon closes his eyes, staggers worse. Stopping, brandishing his fists, at the top of his voice.) God have pity on me!

The scene shows the two men, standing on either side of the tree, each attempting to imitate it, to stand alone with the God-given tree which has grown with them. Astride the mound with the tree between them they resemble the two thieves, so curiously examined by Vladimir in the first moments of the play. Beckett has here made visual and dramatic what Weil left symbolic. Failing to stand alone, failing Godot's presence and the fulfillment of desire, Estragon's only recourse against a distant God is to shout at the top of his voice for pity on his piece of humanity. Not only the characters of this play, but the basic situation, action, and environment, concrete and cosmic reveal the flesh and substance of the predicament of Weil's afflicted.

Waiting for Godot can then be understood as a religious allegory with the catechism provided by Simone Weil. Vladimir and Estragon are anonymous, afflicted souls, incapable either of bettering their situation by action or seeking an answer to their problems by thinking. They wait for God, whom they call Godot, to come to them and, if they accept Him, to plant the seed of salvation in them, which will grow into their tree of life. They have returned, day after day, to this location ("by the tree") which was selected by Godot in a half-remembered earlier meeting; there they stage their game of "doing the tree," in which they recreate the form of an earlier Mound and an earlier Tree. Pozzo stands in contrast to them in this allegory, for he believes that he is marching towards God (St. Saviour) and lays great faith in the powers of education and thought. The second act, however, finds him returning to the same place, apparently still voyaging to St. Saviour but now hopelessly bereft of any thinking knowledge other than insight. This alternate role of man seeking his salvation positively is predictably discounted by Weil, who says, in regard to seeking God, "Even if we were to walk for hundreds of years, we should do no more than go round and round the world." This is of course exactly the path which Pozzo describes, continually returning to the same spot. The Boy comes on his daily task of informing the men that "Godot will not come today but surely tomorrow" and holding out the hope of salvation which is never, in this play, achieved. That the Boy is the Christ of this allegory is obvious—he is Godot's messenger and Vladimir addresses him with the plea "Christ have mercy on us"—but he is much more familiar as a Beckett messiah than as a specific Christian one. A small boy also appears in *Endgame*, holding out the possibility of assistance to the depraved characters in that environment. And at the very end of *Molloy* when the title character, immured in a ditch, hears a voice calling "Don't fret, Molloy, we're coming," that voice sounds to him like "an urchin's thanks."

If we accept that there may be a little Weil in Beckett, we can continue by using *Waiting for God* to help us in discovering the basic ethic and conclusion of *Waiting for Godot*. The ethic must interest us first, for without it we understand nothing of Godot's actions and why he doesn't come. Weil specifically calls for total inaction on man's part if he is to achieve salvation, holding him only liable for an inner obedience and self-enslavement to the system of her universe. Her viewpoint is relentlessly fatalistic:

Men can never escape from obedience to God . . . the only choice given to men . . . is to desire obedience or not to desire it. If a man does not desire it he obeys nevertheless.

Man must give over all selfish interests, all pride, and all identity. He must even give up the "right" of knowledge and questioning:

To empty ourselves of our false divinity, to give up being the center of the world in imagination . . .

To long for God and renounce all the rest, that alone can save us.

Pozzo, in the first act, is furthest of any from the Weil ideals of selflessness. With his concern for prideful adoration and for his personal possessions we may say that his soul is full of false divinity. Only in the second act, when he loses his sight and dignity, does he begin to approach the self-negation which is his final cry. In his two appearances he sandwiches Vladimir and Estragon in degree of affliction, less than they in the first act and considerably more in the second. For the two principles in the play are far from the total renunciation of "all the rest." Estragon has vestiges of his silly pride ("On me! On me! Pity! On me!") and is primarily concerned with being fed, nursing his wounds, and escaping this life. Vladimir is the more noble in his pride, but he cannot forego his questionings of life and attempts to hasten his salvation. His tragedy is the ultimate tragedy of the play; it is basically existential, for he cries out against the meaninglessness of a meaningless universe and tries vainly to determine the patterns and the ethics of an existence which knows neither. He refuses to accept the brutalism of a thoroughly fatalistic life even though his entire existence stands as an unshakeable lesson for it. This is made precise in the first two lines of the play:

ESTRAGON: Nothing to be done.
VLADIMIR: I'm beginning to come round to that opinion. All my life I've tried to put it from me, saying, Vladimir, be reasonable, you haven't yet tried everything. And so I resumed the struggle.

In resuming the struggle he questions religious text, tries to remember proverbs, mulls the possibility of suicide, begs for entertainment from Lucky and then the fallen

Pozzo, and, perhaps worst of all, tries to maintain his rights of inquiry and supplication even knowing that he must willingly and completely give them up. We sense irony rather than faith in his answer to Estragon:

ESTRAGON: We've lost our rights?
VLADIMIR: We got rid of them.

For it is not until he has given up his rights willingly and without resentment, and has declined the struggle, selflessly abandoning himself to the whims of an unjust-seeming God, that God will be able to see him. The action of Vladimir throughout the play is towards a more total self-obliteration which his consciousness rebels against. But, prompted by Pozzo, he gains from the other's insight at the end of the play, leaving the hope of a successful conclusion.

Pozzo's capitulation into affliction is accompanied by a realization of his part of the emptiness of human-ordered existence. In his final speech he attacks the most human, the most logical, and the most necessary fabrication: the man-created institution, time.

POZZO: Have you not done tormenting me with your accursed time? . . . One day he went dumb, one day I went blind, one day we'll go deaf, one day we were born, the same day, the same second. . . . They give birth astride of a grave, the light gleams an instant, then it's night once more.

The words are bleak indeed; gone to mankind, says Pozzo, is time, history, and the earthly joy of life. Life and death are imminently intertwined; life is a moment's insight between two deaths; the history of a man's life is a futile reckoning against meaningless hours and minutes. Vladimir is much moved by this speech, for it is the speech of a man who has in many ways discontinued the struggle and realized what is necessary for the final visit of Godot. Vladimir repeats Pozzo's image and considers it:

VLADIMIR: Astride of a grave and a difficult birth. Down in the hole, lingeringly, the gravedigger puts on the forceps. We have time to grow old. The air is full of our cries. But habit is a great deadener. At me too someone is looking, of me too someone is saying, he is sleeping, he knows nothing, let him sleep on. I can't go on! What have I said?

Vladimir, in crying out "We have time to grow old," is only begging for the ordered run of a man's objectives in living which he is denied in waiting, begging for a history of events he can tie himself to, marked in time against a calendar which he could find. But the insight which Pozzo passes on to him is valuable, and Vladimir too begins to understand in a deeper way the things which he has been wanting to believe all along. The confrontation between the two men is duplicated in the earlier *Molloy* when Moran is retreating to his house for the last time, to return afterwards as Molloy in name as well as spirit. As he nears his home he is accosted by a farmer, resembling in many ways Pozzo. Like Pozzo the farmer wears a bowler, he also is half-recognized by Moran in the same way Pozzo is by Vladimir. Further, his first statement is to question Moran's presence on "his land," which is exactly what Pozzo does. The imagery of Pozzo's final speech, and the meaning, are nearly identical to Moran's description of the farmer:

> He held a lantern in his hand. It was not lit. But he might light it at any moment. In the other hand he held a spade. To bury me with, if necessary.

In this case the realization of Moran that life and death go hand in hand is considered by him important and is about the last thing he relates before his final conversion to the more afflicted Molloy. To Vladimir the message inspires terror and the cry "I can't go on!" But go on he does for the situation is imposed upon him whether he desires it or not, and only this remaining humanness stands between him and his salvation.

Will Godot, though, come at all? If this were a straight parable and the faith of Weil upheld, we must naturally conclude yes. If, however, the story is presented as an ironic fable and shows the predicament of those who place blind faith in a non-existent saviour, then the answer is of course no. And there is no reason to assume that either of these answers is obviously right or wrong since Beckett provides only evidence that Godot does not come during the course of the play. Since this is a play rather than a theological treatise, Beckett is free to set up a theological question and to invest it with the blood of living characters without taking the presumptuous step of answering it. And this is certainly what Beckett has done; he has not "answered" the question, which is the basic question of post-human existence, any more than Shakespeare "answered" Hamlet's famous question, "To be or not to be?" Vladimir and Estragon know as much about Godot as we do about God—we may certainly believe through faith but we have no visual evidence for His existence or His eventual aid to us. *Waiting for Godot* is a Christian parable in Weil's terms that stops just at the point of observed knowledge and does not make faith empirical; rather it throws us back upon our own beliefs. That is why the play means so many things to so many people; Vladimir's destiny is no more sure or unsure than ours. The less-than-startling conclusion is that Godot is in fiction what God is in reality: to the characters Godot is a mixture of belief, hope, fear and doubt; to us and to Beckett God is in varying degrees the same.

If Beckett took from Weil the situation, the characters, and the symbolism, he did not take her ultimate faith. His vision is of man suffering through the bleakness of affliction and enduring it with humor and pathos, always relieved and affrighted with the hope of ultimate salvation. Without this hope there would be no tragedy, for it is this which pins them to their dreadful environment, dreadful because of its terrible uncertainty. Their hope keeps them going but the uncertainty makes them miserable. And neither they, nor the characters outside the play—the audience and the reading public—are offered a ready-made answer to their uncertainty. For Beckett to have offered such would not only have been presumptuous, it would have killed the tragic nature of the play and also abused the audience by easing their minds with a solution they would never accept elsewhere. Shakespeare had the courage and good sense to say "To die and go we know not where," and Beckett the sense to let Godot arrive in an imaginary third, fourth, or *n*th act rather than an actual second.

NOTES

1 G. S. Fraser, "They Also Serve," *TLS*, February 10, 1956, p. 84. This article was published anonymously.
2 *TLS*, April 13, 1956.
3 G. E. Wellwarth, "Life in the Void: Samuel Beckett," *UKCR*, XXVIII: (October 1961), 25-33.
4 Simone Weil, *Waiting for God*, trans. Emma Craufurd (New York: 1959). All quotations from Weil are taken from this edition.
5 Alan Levy, "The Long Wait for Godot," *Theatre Arts* (August 1956), 34. Beckett's quote was made to Alan Schneider, the first American director of *Waiting for Godot*.
6 Hugh Kenner, "The Cartesian Centaur," *Perspective*, XI:3 (Autumn 1959), 132-142. Mr. Kenner has shown how Beckett has used the bicycle as a new foundation for the modern man-centaur, combining the logical geometry of the bicycle with the humanity

of man. I suggest in agreement that the original centaur—half man and half horse—is associated in the minds of Beckett's characters with the deity.

7 Letter to the author, October 5, 1960.

8 Edith Kern, "Moran-Molloy: The Hero As Author," *Perspective*, XI:3 (Autumn 1959), 183-193, is the most convincing example. But the evidence in the novel itself is entirely ample. Moran becomes the character Molloy in every detail, even the elaborate way in which he must ride his bicycle.

9 Proverbs 13:12

CHAPTER

16 On Translating *The Bourgeois Gentleman*

I am not a professional translator. I began translating *The Bourgeois Gentleman* three years ago because I wanted to include several sequences from the play in a book I was writing and I couldn't find a translation that "read funny" enough for my purposes. I also wanted to add stage directions for the reader's benefit, and it seemed rude to graft my own stage directions, in square brackets, to translations made by others—besides, my typewriter could not make square brackets. And finally, I was not all that keen about paying permission fees, particularly since I could not pay them to M. Molière himself. So I translated the sequences. And I found them funny; to paraphrase Jourdain, they were amusing—they amused *me*. So I decided to finish translating the play, and then to produce it.

I am aware of many of the writings on the art of translation: the translator is a traitor, says a euphonious Italian proverb; translation is "the skill of honorable deception,"[1] says William Arrowsmith. "If life begins on the other side of despair," says Eric Bentley, "the translator's life begins on the other side of impossibility."[2] The act of translation has been construed both as an act of criticism ("true translation is much more commentary on the original than a substitute for it,"—D.S. Carne-Ross),[3] and as an independent creative art that may even surpass the original by being "more revealing, closer to the ideal,"[4] according to Jean Paris, whose name is translated as "Gene Paris" or more freely as "Designer Jeans," which are themselves "more revealing and closer to the ideal."

This essay was written for, and delivered at, a 1982 symposium on The Bourgeois Gentlemen *which coincided with my production of the play, which I had also translated, and in which William Needles, a longtime veteran of the Canadian Shakespeare Festival (and a colleague of mine at the University), played Monsieur Jourdain to great acclaim. The translation has since been published: first in a dramatic anthology that I edited (*Eight Plays for Theatre, *Mayfield Publishing Company, 1988), and subsequently in a separate acting edition (Encore Press, 1996).*

The gist of this literature, said over and over in a thousand ways and languages, is that translation is something between a schoolboy crib and a free invention; and that, to be effective, translation must recreate not just the meaning, but the tone, shape, and spirit of the original work. In a comedy, of course, the translation must be comic; in a romance, romantic. In the theatre these require very special applications. Robert Corrigan, a translator of Chekhov as well as a critic and director, writes that "the first law in translating for the theatre is that everything must be speakable. It is necessary for the translator to hear the actor speaking . . . the gestures of the voice . . . the rhythm, the cadence, the interval . . . the look, the feel, and the movement of the actor . . . It is necessary almost to direct the play, act the play, and see the play while translating it."[5] That's very well said, I believe, and it is particularly pertinent to the translator of Molière.

I don't know why Molière has proven so difficult to translate—or, at least, had proven so prior to Richard Wilbur's excellent translations of the past decade and a half. Herma Briffault prefaces her 1957 translation of *The Bourgeois Gentleman* with the comment that the "play has never been adequately translated,"[6] and Roger Shattuck commented some years ago that "of the vast riches of Molière . . . we have only one playable translation . . . Richard Wilbur's *Misanthrope*."[7] No doubt Mr. Shattuck has subsequently come to admire Wilbur's *Tartuffe* and *School for Wives*, as indeed I do, but it is certainly odd that Molière, unquestionably the most popular foreign-language writer on the English-language stage, should have proven such a stumbling block for dedicated Englishifiers.

Molière is, of course, the *homme du théâtre* of incomparable gifts: actor, playwright, director, company manager, and critic; the unequaled master, perhaps, of dramatic mechanics and comic timing. It stands to reason that a successful translator of Molière must have superb theatrical instincts, and there's no question but that this is an area where many translations fail, either through turgidity, lumpishness, preciosity, timidity, or countless other non-theatrical limitations or anti-theatrical inhibitions. Molière is not difficult to translate literally; the French language, after all, has changed little compared to English in the past three centuries, and Molière's working vocabulary was quite small; puny compared to Shakespeare's. Indeed, I first read *The Bourgeois Gentleman* in my eleventh grade French class—the last one I ever took—and I would suggest that, for your typical American high school student, *The Bourgeois Gentleman* is easier to understand in French, than, say, *Measure for Measure* is in English. Clearly, the translator's work on this play is demanding not so much in the task of literal transcription, but in making the piece work on stage.

For what must, after all, be theatricalized in *The Bourgeois Gentleman*? As a comedy-ballet, one turns first to the comedy, then to the dance. Much of the humor is physical. What's funny, after all, about a line like "Fa Fa?" or "Look fierce!" or "Straighten your shoulders?" What's funny, of course, is the way M. Jourdain *says* these lines—or responds to them. The shape of his lips when he says "u." The grimace on his face when he gets up after a bow. What's so funny about the line "Hi hi hi hi hi hi"? (Which I have cleverly translated as "Hee hee hee hee hee hee.") It's funny because the actress is funny, because the acting is funny. This line—and the entire part of Nicole, by the way—was written by Molière especially for the actress Mlle. Beauval, who had been hired entirely on account of her well-known comedic ability to produce an almost unlimited cascade of laughter. The "laughing scene," a familiar *lazzo* from the *commedia dell'arte*, is typical of the untranslatable theatricality of Molière: untranslatable simply because it does not need to be translated, it needs to be created; the juxtaposition of Nicole's riotous laughter and Jourdain's rage-suppressing scowls creates a humor (and meaning) that derives from mime, not language, and from a theatre where gesture reigns, at least at this moment, supreme.

Thus the first challenge of translating *this* play, it seems to me, is to set up the physical juxtapositions, the "sight gags," and the context where ballets, songs, scantily motivated entrances, and arbitrary plot turns can be entertainingly accommodated. And that, without question, means a control of timing. Timing is always crucial in the theatre, but it is one of the first things to be lost in translation, particularly in translation between French and English, which Jean Paris calls "the two most incomparable . . . most incompatible tongues of the Western World."[8] French is a tighter language than English, with fewer words and fewer sounds: editors estimate that an English translation of a French work will run an average of 20% longer.[9] This may be why a recent production of *The Bourgeois Gentleman* ran three hours compared to our two: the attempt to pin down every nuance of the French text forced a corresponding sacrifice of the French rhythms. Semantic exactitude, in stage realizations, often means that the timing is shot, the play lengthened, the comedy killed, and the audience wearied; surely *theatrical* exactitude—or equivalence—should have preference when preference must be found.

The second challenge is to find a way to place the play in a cultural context which contains both the courtly circle of King Louis XIV, who commissioned the work, and the modern audience who is paying to see it; this is a director's responsibility in any case. Yet any attempt to reduce this process to a logical method is, in my opinion, doomed. Rationalists looking for an easy answer could request a "pure" historical version; modernists could demand a wholesale update; neither is terribly felicitous. We necessarily bring the play into modern times simply by turning our electric lights on it, seating our audience in comfortable theatre seats, and allowing the production to be viewed by contemporary eyes and sensibilities. And yet, complete modernizing would inevitably trivialize the context. Nor can we satisfactorily go "in between," as if, by striking a balance between 1671 and 1982 and setting the play in 1826, we had successfully achieved midpoint. No, like a marriage, the translation will have something old, something new, something borrowed, and something blue, and in this case *The Bourgeois Gentleman*'s translation will include some of the potpourri of styles that the original audaciously demonstrated.

I have done a great deal of lifting—"something borrowed"—in the translation, following Molière's own precept that he would take, for his own, whatever he could find elsewhere. You may note in my translation certain literary borrowings: from Shakespeare, Proust, Keats, Milton, Ecclesiastes, and Samuel Beckett. I've included these quotations not simply as gags, nor to enter the critical realms of intertextuality, but simply to give the text a certain resonance by fitting it into a cultural context; a literary consanguinity that the original possessed, and no contemporary version could or should ignore. In other words, the literary references (most of which will have a subliminal effect, if any) are not meant to be satirical anachronisms, conscious updatings, or cheap gags, but rather gentle references that continually remind the audience that this is a work solidly lodged in the center of our cultural heritage, and that the past foibles of the 17th century French court are exemplars of quite universal behavior. We are, after all, still in the Renaissance, and consistency to any one year or decade or century within that epoch is not, as far as I can see, of critical importance except to literary accountants. Molière blended Roman comedy, Renaissance neoclassicism, and slapstick *commedia* in this play with a lighthearted joyousness that we cannot but find engaging, and I have equally delightedly collated a number of new sources from succeeding generations which I do not feel compromise Molière's spirit in any way at all.

The text is in prose, and is at some times quite abrupt; an abruptness which Americans are often surprised to find in Molière, and assume to be the argot of the translator. Albert Bermel, a fine Molière translator complains that "many translators are tempted to shy away from (Molière's) roughness, to purge him, comb his hair when it looks unruly, and clean him up; these are affronts . . . You end up with a polite English tone which is not a true equivalent . . . (making) Molière read and sound like

a watered-down Restoration comedy."[10] I have used many contemporary sayings—
"Are we gonna buy this?" for example, and "What's the story this time?"—but have
tried to keep a clean line that is neither wholly modern, nor wholly vernacular, nor
elaborately flowery; instead I have used all these tones as I believe Molière used them,
as appropriate to different situations.

Thus the dramaturgically "mechanical" build of the lovers' reunion escalates from
the simple:

    —Well, then explain.
    —No, I've said enough.
    —Tell me.
    —No, I have nothing to tell.

to the more formal:

    —Have a heart.
    —No.
    —I beg you.
    —Leave me alone.
    —I implore you.
    —Go away from me.

to the rhetorically over-inflated:

    —Speak to me!
    —Absolutely not!
    —Enlighten my suspicians!
    —I can't be bothered.
    —Ameliorate my anxiety!
    —I have no wish to do so.

So much for something old and something new: as far as barbarisms, or "something blue," I will cite Richard Wilbur's introduction to his translation of *The
Misanthrope*: "There are occasional vulgarities, but for these there is precedent in the
original, Molière's people being aristocrats, and therefore not genteel."[11] The charac-

ters in *The Bourgeois Gentleman* are not aristocrats, save for Dorante and Dorimene, therefore I have not used any vulgarities except those of incongruities, with the exception of a couple of "hells" and one "dammit" that escape M. Jourdain. For Madame Jourdain's "Chansons!" which my *Dictionary of French Slang* and most of the play's translators render as "Stuff and Nonsense!", I have coined the expletive "Bulldirt!" which I think treads the line between aggravated obscenity and feminine restraint, and also packs the two syllable punch of the original: I hope the word enters the English language, as I find it more powerful than its commoner synonym.

I have used alliteration and verbal sounds wherever possible, and tried to maintain the momentum of the French text—the sonic momentum—wherever I could. This has often been fun:

> Curse the tailor, keeping me waiting all day . . . May malaria mangle him! May the plague pickle him! A detestable tailor, a devilish tailor, a dog of a tailor, a traitorous tailor, a—ah, there you are tailor, I was just about to get angry at you.

Compare with the more literal Briffault translation:

> That cursed tailor keeps me waiting when I have so much to do! May the quartan fever shake that tormentor of a tailor! To the devil with the tailor. May the plague choke the tailor. If I had him here now, that detestable tailor, I'd . . . Oh, you're here? I was getting in a rage against you.[12]

I might mention a couple of things about the Briffault translation in contrast. "May the quartan fever shake that tormentor of a tailor" is quite correct, but almost impossible to read with any force; the emphasis is even throughout, and the invective climaxes on a blandly stressed three-syllable insult—"tormentor"—which makes a feeble cap to the sonic thrust of the accusation. The moment when Jourdain discovers the tailor is also less than it should be: "I'd—oh, you're here" is an abrupt shift between consonant and vowel, whereas "a—ah, there you are" allows Jourdain to comically elide between invective and welcome with an embarassed laugh. (In French, the elision is "je—ah, vous voilà!"). Finally, in Briffault, Jourdain simply confirms what we have seen with his "I was getting in a rage against you;" in the French, Jourdain says *"je m'allais mettre en colere contre vous,"*—"I was *just about* to get angry with you," which is, of course, a little fib, indicating Jourdain's unwillingness to confront the tailor—a tailor to the court—with his ire; a fib which shows us Jourdain's fundamental insecurity, a pertinent aspect of his character.

I have emphasized the comedic aspects of the translation because *The Bourgeois Gentleman* is so dominantly a performance piece; by all accounts a hasty welding of two plays Molière was working on when Louis commissioned an entertainment following the hunt at Chambord. Anyone who has visited the hunt country around Chambord—a countryside something like our rural West Virginia—knows that it is one of the wildest regions of Western Europe, and that the entertainment of hunters in that region—even royal hunters—would not ordinarily turn to character nuances and literary delicacies. In *The Bourgeois Gentleman* there is virtually no plot, no character development, and the principal characters, save for the title character himself, are not even introduced until the third act—following two songs and three ballets. The endurance of this comedy-ballet is, however, astonishing; it has been presented regularly by the Comédie Française for more than three centuries (there has been no decade since its writing when it has not been revived by that troupe) and has been translated and produced all over the world. Clearly the satirical basis of the comedy is universal; clearly it touches us in many ways. Perhaps that universality comes from the fact that Molière, deep down, is satirizing himself. There could not have been a soul in the original audience that did not know that M. Jourdain, the play's dunce, was performed by M. Molière, the play's author; and probably not a soul was unaware that Molière, himself, was a bourgeois gentleman: the son of an upholsterer and the favorite of the King's court. But there are other targets for Molière's deft jabs: the "paytrones of the ahts" that the Music Master derides must include the King's brother, who guided Molière out of the provinces and into the King's favor—and possibly even the King himself, who organized plays and ballets for the entertainment of his friends and mistresses, kept a retinue of singers and dancers at his beck and call, and even performed (badly? we do not know) in some of Molière's musical works. Can we not see King Louis XIV doing the minuet to the instructions of the Dancing Master, or donning the turban (the crown?) as the Mammamouchi? Is this Louis' insecurity we are seeing across the ages? We will never know, but it is told that Louis refused to speak after the play's premiere, allowing the courtiers to infer his displeasure; only the next day did he tell Molière that the piece was as good as anything the dramatist had ever written.

Or is the play about us? Do we see Nancy Reagan's china at the bourgeois banquet table? Closer to home, the philosopher's lesson could be, word for word, the instruction in a Speech for Actors class. The sound "u" *is* "made up by bringing the teeth together, by spreading the lips, and then making them come together without quite touching." If there's an edge of exaggeration in this satire, I can't find it; nor can I find it in the tailor scene—in an age when Ralph Lauren sells us (or sells somebody) shredded denim jackets for $500 ("You never told me you wanted it without rips!") and where designer jeans, which, as I have said need no translating, are a worldwide phenomenon.

Clearly, *The Bourgeois Gentleman* has resonances of the old and the new, of the borrowed and the blue, which come through in the resonances of past and present, French and English, elegant and coarse that I have left in and put into the translation. But the most profound resonance is, as always with this author, with the universal strivings of our species: our delights and bewilderments at art, love, learning, and family; our mystification in the face of language, our groping confrontation with the demands of society and social position, and our joy in discovering, after all these years, that we have indeed been speaking prose all of our lives.

NOTES

1 William Arrowsmith & Roger Shattuck, eds, *The Craft and Context of Translation* (Austin, TX: 1961), p. 125.

2 *Ibid.*, p. 105.

3 *Ibid.*, p. 6.

4 *Ibid.*, p. 63.

5 *Ibid.*, p. 101.

6 Molière, *The Middle-Class Gentleman*, trans. by Herma Briffault (Woodbury, NY: 1957), p. 6.

7 William Arrowsmith & Roger Shattuck, *op. cit.*, p. 192.

8 *Ibid.*, p. 58.

9 *Ibid.*, p. 169.

10 *One-Act Comedies of Molière*, trans. by Albert Bermel (Cleveland, OH: 1965), p. 11.

11 *The Misanthorpe and Tartuffe*, trans. by Richard Wilbur (New York: 1965), p. 10.

12 Briffault, *op. cit.*, p. 36.

CHAPTER

17 The Doctors in Spite of Themselves

It is a modern play, simply staged on a bare floor, with polished wooden benches that pivot to indicate the shifting locales. As the lights come up, a brief pantomime hints at a story to come; then a man, a professional therapist, advances toward the audience and begins a soliloquy. His life, he explains, is in a state of confusion. There has been, you see, this extraordinary patient . . .

Flashback. A colleague is entering with a referral. There is, he says, this extraordinary patient . . . whom nobody else has been able to handle. The therapist stalls. His schedule, he explains, is already overbooked. Still, there is something intriguing about this case . . .

The patient enters. It is the character we saw in the pantomime: sullen, angry, unspeaking. The therapist attempts a few jokes to break the ice; there is, in response, only the grimmest of glares. The therapist provokes his patient with a cutting remark; there is connection, but no communication. This will be slow work!

The therapist visits the patient's mother's home, searching for clues, but "Mom" is unforthcoming, and bursts into defensive hostility at the mention of sexual matters. The therapist somberly returns to his patient—but now comes a peculiar shift. The patient's world, the therapist discovers, is intensely rich with private fantasy; it is filled with elegant symbols and vivid rituals, fascinating in their originality and wholeness. The patient, it appears, is an artist of the unconscious, while the therapist, by contrast, begins to feel himself sterile of imagination, a man tightly bound in spiritual knots.

The therapist begins to doubt: is it proper to "adjust" his patient to the barren world he himself inhabits? The therapist reflects back onto the distant and primitive civilizations he has recently visited across the seas—places where heroism seemed more precisely defined, and where divinity and adventure seemed closer to day-to-day life than they are in the therapist's professional milieu. The therapist decides that his life, in contrast to his patient's, is ruled by lesser deities and more prosaic realities. He begins to *admire* his patient, and pretty soon that admiration becomes an emotional attachment.

Gradually, the roles reverse: the patient begins to treat the therapist!

Eventually, as his colleagues advise, and as his cultural bias demands, the therapist provokes a confrontation with his patient, forcing an explosive re-enactment of past trauma which, we are given to understand, becomes the first step towards the patient's "recovery." This is also a moment of great stage climax providing the theatre audience a dramaturgical catharsis just as it provides the patient a psychotherapeutic (even psychodramatic) one.

But the play is not yet over. As the patient recedes into the background, echoing the opening pantomime, the therapist advances towards us a final time, and concludes his opening soliloquy. The patient, he explains, may not really be recovering at all. The issues are not in fact resolved. Human beings, the therapist concludes, remain alone in darkness and silence. And this darkness and silence are reinforced by the dimming of the stage lights as the play comes to an end.

Of course this description is of Peter Shaffer's award-winning play, *Equus*. And, of course, it is also of Mark Medoff's award winning-play, *Children of a Lesser God*. The structures of the two plays, to the extent they are described above, are absolutely identical in all particulars.

The structural identity, while probably coincidental,[1] is somewhat astonishing. Yet there are also consonances, if not identities, with several other modern dramas, such as Bernard Pomerance's *The Elephant Man* and Arthur Kopit's *Wings*. In all these plays the "doctor" figure—the therapist—comes to see himself or herself as less spiritually developed less creative, less fully realized than the outwardly aberrant "patient" figure. There is a pattern here, and a pattern that may be shown to have some historical roots—as well as some contemporary implications.

I would like to isolate three different treatments of the "doctor" in drama, without making any claim to an all-inclusive or universally exclusive categorization. These three treatments seem to have been developed chronologically, and I shall list them in that order.

Sureness, coupled with wholly good intentions, characterized the first doctors portrayed in Western drama. Tiresias, the Greek prophet, seer, and witch-doctor, received his arts from the gods, and his methodology from inspiration; he cured the Theban plague by diagnosing its cause and indicating the cure—which was to expunge the city's polluting member. Likewise, the doctors of medieval drama, who, acting on divine authority, concluded morality plays with high-toned summaries and moral lessons, were absolute in their assumptions, firm in their judgments, and noble in their sentiments; like Tiresias, they were "knowers" more than medical practitioners.

On stage, the doctor as knower soon evolved into the doctor as hero. As experimental empiricism, innovative technology and a highly sophisticated pharmacology replaced inspiration and divine law as therapeutic guideposts, the modern stage doctor became a scientific warrior. Doctor-heros dominated mid-century American drama, curing yellow fever (*Yellowjack*), making the crippled walk (*Sunrise at Campobello*), and teaching the deaf to speak *(The Miracle Worker)*. In early television, Marcus Welby, Doctor Kildare, Ben Casey, and the white-cloaked denizens of TV soap operas became the "good doctors" who nurtured Americans back to physical health, much as Tiresias and the medieval play-enders provided their audiences with spiritual confirmation and renewal.

There have always been "bad doctors" on our stages, however. These have mainly been those ambitious creatures who, seeking knowledge beyond the human province, have transcended normal human aspirations. Marlowe's Doctor Faustus is a prototype here, followed by Doctor Frankenstein, Doctor Jekyll, and the host of villain-physicians that populate subgenres such as vaudeville (Dr. Kronkeit) and American horror films (*Coma*) right up to the present day. In most twentieth century drama, of course, the intellectual overreaching of the bad doctor was no longer merely construed as against an assault on religion, but on humanity and humanistic values: the white-coated doctors of Tennessee Williams, for example, as they cart Blanche to the asylum in *Streetcar,* or administer truth serum in *Suddenly Last Summer,* represent not the anti-Christ but the increased impersonality of modern medical professions. And the disembodied voice that questions patients in Michael Christofer's *The Shadow Box,* the interchangeable and largely inanimate physicians hectoring their patient/victims in Brian Clark's *Whose Life is it Anyway?* and Peter Nichols' *The National Health,* and the chorus of doctors and residents who privilege research priorities over patient comfort in Margaret Edson's *Wit* are certainly not evil antagonists, yet they clearly represent a diminution of what earlier eras expected in the way of human compassion. So while doctor-as-villain is pretty much left to the melodramas, today's dramatic physician is often seen, if through a narrow or hyperbolic focus, as an abstract of institutional oppression.

Yet the good/bad and hero/villain dichotomies do not limit the most intriguing pattern of dramatic physician characterizations, and the two plays of the 1970s described in the initial paragraphs of this essay deal with a sort of professional complexity and moral ambiguity that is worth further exploration. These plays treat the limits of medical and even scientific limits.

Limits, of course, are empirical facts, defined by the current state of knowledge. "This disease is beyond my practice," says Lady Macbeth's physician. But the quest for health and healing knows no empirical boundaries, and the physician of every age must contend with the patient's deeply seated expectation of a divinely delivered cure—as well as the patient's fear of medical malignity. Between Tiresias and Frankenstein stands the medical practitioner, in his or her self-esteem, public image, and dramaturgical "role."

Molière provided the subtitle for this genre, which is also the title of this essay. In *The Doctor In Spite of Himself,* Moilère depicts the uneducated bumpkin, Sganarelle, who, despite his protestations to the contrary, is mistaken by country folk for a physician. As the yokels insist on bringing patients to him, Sganarelle finally—to get rid of them if nothing else—begins to diagnose and treat them. Lo and behold, his treatments become cures; eventually he starts charging fees, swaggering a bit, and enjoying his new profession. The state of medical knowledge being what it was at the, time, Molière enjoys his little joke: that a bumpkin well as a royal physician can cure boils. The play, of course, is a farce, but it does pose an interesting semantic question: is Sganarelle "really" a doctor? To be sure, Sganarelle has no training nor certification, but the fact remains that he does diagnose, treat, and cure: in other words, he *doctors.* If one is one's acts and nothing else, as Sartre maintains, then Sganarelle is a doctor (if in spite of himself) both by definition and by practice.

We need not take Sganarelle's dilemma, nor its inherent semantic question, very seriously; we cannot, however, lightly dismiss the problem of Goethe's Faust:

> The crowd's applause now sounds like scorn to me . . .
> Here was the medicine: the patients died
> And no one questioned . . .
> I gave the poison unto thousands, ere
> They pined away: and I must live to hear
> The shameless murderers praised and blessed.

Faust—and his father, hence the plural "murderers"—is, unlike Sganarelle, a trained doctor, but his attempted cure turns out to be worse than the disease, and his patients, ignorant of his failure, die blessing their killer. While the ignoramus

Sganarelle practices good medicine and the educated Faust practices bad, both see themselves as charlatans; both privately rue the public approbation wrongly heaped upon their acts. Both are widely viewed as miracle workers and both know they have no miracles to deliver.

The model is extended into the beginning of this century by Anton Chekhov, himself a doctor as well as a playwright, who puts these words in the mouth of Chebutykin:

> They think I'm a doctor, that I know how to cure any
> kind of sickness. I know absolutely nothing . . .
> Last Wednesday I treated a woman in Sasyp. She died,
> and it's my fault she died. Yes . . .I used to know
> a thing or two twenty-five years ago, and now I
> remember nothing!
>
> *(Three Sisters)*

Chebutykin, while neither farcical nor Faustian, shares the dissonance between his own sense of identity and his public reputation; in spite of themselves, these doctors are compelled to carry on. The Sganarelle-Faust-Chebutykin model, spanning three centuries and three dramatic modes, is a testament to human futility in the face of human suffering: the limits of medical science versus the illimitable life force, and the quest for health and survival.

The later years of the present century have brought a medical revolution and an educated populace, and the dramatic issue in plays treating the ambiguity of medical intervention has turned from an exploration of charlatanism to an examination of the nature of health, and, by extention, the curative process itself. This has led to the model posited at the beginning of this essay.

The limits of medicine are now widely known, to practioner and practionee alike. The subjectivity of objective science—in an age when even physics is governed by a principle of uncertainty—has turned the practice of medical therapy into a virtual partnership between doctor and client, rather than the imposition of the divine, the esoteric, or the occult by a good, bad, or charlatanical physician. And, in the contem-porary theatrical realization of this practice, a curious dramatic shift of focus has occurred. Instead of seeing the doctor as knower/curer, we now tend to see the patient in this role. More and more, in contemporary theatre, the patient has begun to treat the therapist, and the therapist has begun to kneel at the altar of the patient.

One sees this contemporary shift beginning, perhaps, in Peter Weiss' remarkably epochal *Marat/Sade,* a play of tremendous influence owing to the Peter Brook stage production and film, seen widely throughout the world in the late 1960s. Ken Kesey's novel *One Flew Over the Cuckoo's Nest,* popularized in both stage and film versions during the early 1970s, was also a key factor. Both works were set in mental institutions; both portrayed the medical establishment (psychiatric in each case) as essentially malign—not by plan but by lack of plan. Both strongly suggested the theory, supported in psychiatric literature by British psychiatrist R. D. Laing, that medical intervention was more likely to cause than to cure mental illness. The Weiss and Kesey works were followed by plays that moved beyond the psychiatric to the more conventionally medical, plays which questioned purely medical approaches to various physical ailments: deformity in *The Elephant Man,* obesity in *Transmogrification of Benno Blimpie,* stroke in *Wings,* paralysis in *Whose Life Is It Anyway?,* cancer in *The National Health, Wit* and *Shadow Box* and deafness and psychosis in the two plays cited at the beginning of this essay. In each of these plays, the author has explored the question of malignancy in normal healthiness: the illness of the doctor, or therapist, or medical establishment. The Normal is the truly sick.

"The Normal is the indispensable, murderous God of Health, and I am his Priest," says Dr. Dysart in *Equus,* in what might represent a defining statement of the motif. Dysart's capitalized "Normal" is a biological impersonality raised to divine status; it is an inhuman norm defined by statistics refined by computer analysis, and stamped out—or stamped in—by less and less willing medical experts. Against this deified Normal are the defiantly abnormal: the enlightened sick. They include the architects of make-believe cathedrals like the Elephant Man; those who speak through the eloquent language of gesture and sign, like Sarah in *Children of a Lesser God*; those who make sublime if disoriented and aphasaic poetry, like Mrs. Stilson in *Wings*; and those who, like Alan Strang in *Equus,* live a life of blazing, brilliant, wonderfully enviable passion when all about them is a life of quiet despair. The milder neurotics of Tennessee Williams have been superceded by the catatonics (Peter Weiss), the schizophrenics (Peter Shaffer), and the paralytics (Peter Nichols); these are the new heroes, the sympathetic protagonists of a new dramatic genre.

To the dramatist, ever an individualist, a dialectic between the healthy world of Normal, on the one hand, and a sickly magnificance on the other, is entirely one-sided. Magnificence has always had its audience, and Normalcy, since Warren

Harding, has been utterly discredited in the public eye. The audience's sympathies, at least in the Western world of the 1980s, are on the side of the unique, the perverse, the Special; that is certainly where the excitement is, and those intelligent therapists saddled with the job of "curing" magnificence can only do so with an overwhelming sense of shame.

But in the shame is a new dramatic model—one very much in keeping with our times. If the patient is not the genius, it is a genius which we can only admire: we cannot share it or accept it into our lives. And therefore our identification turns to the doctor: not as an expert—good, bad, or charlatanical—but as an individual, a confrere, facing a particularly universal crisis. We are no longer chiefly concerned with the patient's illness, but rather with the doctor's concern with the patient's illness. We are concerned with the meta-problem of the Doctor's Dilemma: how to reconcile the Normal with the Special. It is not a concern that is foreign to the general theatre audience, which accounts for the great popularity of these mentioned plays. The doctor is the anti-hero. The doctor is us.

What I think we are dealing with most fundamentally in these plays is the intractable limits to knowledge and experience and—for want of a better word—transcendence in human life; and the inability of professionalism—either in medicine or in any other field—to crack those limits. The modern theatre audience sees itself as a professional elite.

Demographic studies in Europe (East and West) and America make that clear—so does any common-sense analysis of ticket prices on Broadway and in the regional theatres. Playwrights themselves can share in this general affluence—and most of the cited plays were written by authors already established at the time of writing. In general, the audience may admire the patient/victim of these plays, but will identify with the wealthy professional and his Faustian problems of self-assurance. The medical model has succeeded because doctors are simply our most common (most admired, most feared) professionals; therefore our best representatives of our own discomforture at the excessive Normality of our lives, and our lack of Specialness before the universe. We have, as a class (the professional class, the theatre-going class), come to despise the sterility that makes us "well," and the dispassion of professional relationships that makes them "objective." We are in an age in which we sense quite precisely the blandness of professional intercourse and the hollowness of professional prestige. It is a world in which hospital corridors, as well as the halls of academe, bulge with doctors in spite of themselves, daydreaming of greater deities to serve. The generally pessimistic endings of these plays indicates that the search will go on.

NOTES

1 Medoff has said he is not aware aware of any influence from *Equus,* the earlier play, on *Children.* Private discussion, February 3, 1984.

CHAPTER

18 Rude Awakening

"Why should I wake up? This dream is going so well!" So sings the young American visitor to prewar Berlin in Kander and Ebb's *Cabaret*, and the lyric has reverberated through my head since September 11. For the American dream was going very well, particularly in New York City, until that day. Under the strict anti-crime administration of Mayor Guiliani, the city's homicide rate had been cut nearly in half, to less than two a day, within a mere decade; then, in an instant, 3,000 murders devastated lower Manhattan. The Broadway theatre, having just completed its greatest year in history, went suddenly dark, with seven shows announcing immediate closings and the rest facing near-empty houses. The long-awaited Broadway premiere of Steven Sondheim's *Assassins*, about to go into rehearsal, was aborted. All commercial airplanes—in the country that both makes and flies more of them than any other—were immediately grounded; within a day rumors (and within a week, evidence) of bioterror caused widespread fear and the grounding of all crop dusting aircraft. The U.S. stock market took its greatest point-fall in history.

The awakening was not immediate. President George W. Bush, reading to Texas schoolchildren when word of the second tower attack reached him, remained chatting with the children for a full six minutes; it was like hitting the presidential snooze button for just a few more winks before facing the dreadful new morning in America. And when the president spoke publicly for the first time, he still seemed dazed. Most of us spent the hideous day staring at our television sets in near-disbelief. Children, coming of age after the Cold War and bombing of Iraq, were stunned beyond measure.

And now America, fully awake, faces a profoundly changed environment. Retaliation and counter-retaliation are ongoing in many parts of the world, reported everywhere in the media and cyberspace.

Originally published as *Das Unsanfte Erwache*, in *Theater der Zeit*, November 2001

Some aspects of life are, of course, returning to something resembling normal—or what normal used to be. The airplanes are flying with increasing passenger loads (though more air-scares like the hoax in Delhi and the Sibir downing in the Black Sea may reverse this); the stock market regained most of its immediate losses (though uncertainty about the "new war" promises further damage); and a small portion of front-page newspaper space gave way last week to Barry Bonds's breaking baseball's home-run record.

And the theatre has returned to New York. "White Way roaring back" reported the trade paper *Variety* two weeks after the attack, and all but a few Broadway shows—those few long-running hits now mainly dependent on tourist audiences—have recaptured most of their pre-11/9 attendance. Some, like *The Allergist's Wife*, a rather clever comedy, have actually exceeded it. Two of the shows that had announced their closings (*Kiss Me Kate, The Music Man*) decided to reopen after all. Both *The Lion King* and *The Producers* are again playing to standing room only, and Strindberg's uncannily appropriate *Dance of Death*, along with Ibsen's *Hedda Gabler*, are headed for very strong Broadway openings. (Astonishingly, ticket sales for *Dance of Death* were more than double that of tourist-dependent *Les Miserables* last week.) A 25% salary concession by the theatre unions that helped generate the rebound has, in fact, been already reduced from the planned four weeks to two, and, short of fresh attacks on U.S. soil, is likely to be over by the time you read this. Off- and off-off-Broadway are also back to near-normal; *Bat Boy*, which had announced its closing the day of the events has already announced its reopening, though with a reduced performing schedule. And regional theatres around the country have, for the most part, stabilized, with close-to-normal business in all but the largest venues. Many regional companies have created special programs in the weeks following the attacks, with staging readings from both relevant dramas (e.g., Mark Antony's "bleeding piece of earth" speech in *Julius Caesar*, any number of speeches from *Trojan Women*) and historical texts (Lincoln's Gettysburg address, Franklin Roosevelt's "day of infamy" speech to Congress in 1941), to reassure their subscribers and friends (and, perhaps most important, their own company members) that theatre has a role to play in creating public communion and assuaging public anxiety.

But what about the *character* of American theatre? Can it assume a larger role in the current public discourse? Can it fulfill its historic global function as a forum for social debate? Can it provide, as Euripides' *Trojan Women* must have done during the Peloponnesian War, Anouilh's *Antigone* during the Nazi occupation of Paris, or *Uncle*

Tom's Cabin during America's long struggle with slavery, dramatic models for analyzing current crises?

Mainstream American drama has, to this point, barely touched upon the global issues brought to sudden and overwhelming public attention on September 11. The last decade of Pulitzer Prize-winning plays—the cream of our national crop—have dealt almost entirely with internal family matters: divorce and friendship (*Dinner With Friends*); near-incest (*How I Learned to Drive*); family relations (*Proof, Three Tall Women, Young Man From Atlanta, Lost in Yonkers, Kentucky Cycle, Fences, The Piano Lesson*); or extended family relations (*Angels in America, Driving Miss Daisy, Rent*). Racial issues surface in many of these plays (*Fences, Daisy, Piano Lesson, Angels)* and domestic politics (plus a lot more) in several others (*Kentucky, Angels*), while *Wit* treats the important dialectic between medical research and medical treatment, but absolutely none of these plays, and few others in our recent national repertoire (Lee Blessing's *A Walk in the Woods* is a rare exception) concentrate at all on matters of international geopolitical struggles or global concerns.

It's no wonder we've been dreaming; in general, Americans have been culturally hibernating in a cave far more isolated than Mr. Osama Bin Laden's. A year ago, the presidentially-created Gilmore Commission reported the "stark realization that a terrorist attack on some level within our borders is inevitable," but very few—in the public or media—paid serious attention. Not long before that, a commission on airport security headed by Vice President Al Gore recommended 31 crucial measures to protect air travel; almost none have been fully implemented. And former Defense Secretary William Cohen's 1998 declaration that "the challenge of terrorism demands that we think the unthinkable—attacks with weapons of mass destruction on American soil," was almost completely ignored, as the national media seemed almost wholly preoccupied with political sex scandals, amusement park accidents, and domestic shark attacks. So it is little wonder that the American theatre world has been mainly focused on dysfunctional families.

Well, we've awakened. There seems little doubt that the scope of American drama will move further from home in the coming year, and probably beyond. But how and in what direction? Surely there will be a search for dramas, new and old, that seek to cross the great cultural divides—geographic, cultural, linguistic, and religious—and the terrors and warfare that so often mark the eruptions of those divides. These are dramatic topics relatively unseen here for the past decades, except when coming from abroad in plays by, for instance, Bertolt Brecht, Ariel Dorfman, Harold Pinter, Tom

Stoppard, Brian Friel, Michael Frayn, David Hare, David Edgar, or, good heavens, even William Shakespeare. We have almost no recent American equivalents, say, for *Mother Courage, Death and the Maiden, One for the Road, Indian Ink, Travesties, Translations, Copenhagen, Via Dolorosa, Pentecost,* or even *Antony and Cleopatra, Coriolanus* or *Henry V.*

And we should, I hope, be seeing plays that question our favorite dramatic subject, the "American dream" as already bashed and pilloried by Eugene O'Neill, Arthur Miller, and a thousand other American dramatists, but plays which can also address the global and not merely domestic aspects of our American ideals, naiveté, and might.

"We're considering plays that dramatize the need for tolerance under pressure, plays that question totalitarian and imperialistic minds, works that cry out for inclusion, and that question what it means to be American: who we are as a People, what's good, and what's not working in our culture," says Simon Levy, producing director of the Los Angeles Fountain Theatre.

"Let's hope the theatre will be used as a forum to address the fears and issues we're facing," said Des McAnuff of the La Jolla Playhouse. "I think we'll do the same plays we would have done, but with a greater awareness of the resonances they will carry for our audiences," says Jerry Patch, head of the literary department at South Coast Repertory. All of these words are more or less echoed by many regional theatre directors around the country this month.

Assassins has already been rescheduled for its Broadway opening early next year. Though not a play of global perspective, it is a stirring piece of musical theatre that dramatizes the dialectics of political assassination and the resulting terrors and uncertainties. Little else is known for sure, but I hope the literary managers in New York and around the country heed the calls of those I've cited here, and start digging through their files and dramatic libraries to hunt down—in addition to the usual entertainments and diversions—edgy and performable works addressing matters of a far larger scope and scale than we have been accustomed to. Tony Kushner, well ahead of the curve with his brand new *Homebody/Kabul* (opening in New York on December 19), and with *Slavs!* already on the boards in several cities, is certainly leading the way. And perhaps someone in the theatre's import business will think to bring over one of Ariane Mnouchkine's productions of Hélène Cixous's far-ranging works of historic East-West confrontations (Cixous' *Norodom Sihanouk* has indeed played recently at a college in Illinois). Or at least we might have another go-around of Peter Brook's *Mahabharata.*

And perhaps the American public might demand its theatres, both great and small, seek and commission new American plays that, unlike the general current repertoire, search beyond the mere inconsistencies of our domestic arrangements, and look with vision toward the grave global challenges that now face us all.